Cultural Intelligence

CULTURAL
INTELLIGENCE

Surviving and Thriving in the
Global Village
THIRD EDITION

DAVID C. THOMAS

and

KERR INKSON

BK

Berrett–Koehler Publishers, Inc.
a BK Business book

Berrett-Koehler Publishers, Inc.
1333 Broadway, Suite 1000
Oakland, CA 94612-1921
Tel: (510) 817-2277; Fax: (510) 817-2278
www.bkconnection.com

Ordering Information

Quantity sales. Special discounts are available on quantity purchases by corporations, associations, and others. For details, contact the "Special Sales Department" at the Berrett-Koehler address above.

Individual sales. Berrett-Koehler publications are available through most bookstores. They can also be ordered directly from Berrett-Koehler: Tel: (800) 929-2929; Fax: (802) 864-7626; www.bkconnection.com

Orders for college textbook/course adoption use. Please contact Berrett-Koehler: Tel: (800) 929-2929: Fax: (802) 864-7626.

Distributed to the U.S. trade and internationally by Penguin Random House Publisher Service

Berrett-Koehler and the BK logo are registered trademarks of Berrett-Koehler Publishers, Inc.

Printed in the United States of America

Berrett-Koehler books are printed on long-lasting acid-free paper. When it is available, we choose paper that has been manufactured by environmentally responsible processes. These may include using trees grown in sustainable forests, incorporating recycled paper, minimizing chlorine in bleaching, or recycling the energy produced at the paper mill.

Library of Congress Cataloging-in-Publication Data
Names: Thomas, David C. (David Clinton), 1947–   author. | Inkson, Kerr, author.
Title: Cultural intelligence : surviving and thriving in the global village / David C. Thomas and Kerr Inkson.
Description: Third Edition. | Oakland : Berrett-Koehler Publishers, Inc., [2017] | Revised edition of the authors' Cultural intelligence, c2009. | Includes bibliographical references and index.
Identifiers: LCCN 2016045117 | ISBN 9781626568655 (pbk.)
Subjects: LCSH: Intercultural communication. | Cultural awareness. | Crosscultural orientation.
Classification: LCC HM1211 .T486 2017 | DDC 306--dc23 LC record available at https://lccn.loc.gov/2016045117

THIRD EDITION
24 23 22 21 20 19   10 9 8 7 6 5 4 3 2

Produced and designed by BookMatters, copyedited by Tanya Grove, proofread by Janet Reed Blake, indexed by Leonard Rosenbaum, and cover designed by Dan Tesser, Studio Carnelian

*To the champions of diversity
in all nations*

Contents

Preface

Cultural intelligence is a critical skill in surviving and thriving in today's global environment. In the second edition we applied cultural intelligence broadly to people's interactions not just in organizations but in their daily lives. In this third edition we focus on how to develop this critical ability.

We are reminded daily of the globally interconnected world in which we live. Events on one side of the globe reverberate instantaneously on the other. Globalization has many effects, but one of the most important is the dramatic increase in the opportunity and need to interact with people who are culturally different from us. We are exposed on a daily basis to a wide variety of attitudes, values, beliefs, and assumptions that culturally different individuals hold about appropriate behavior. In order to solve the problems of today's global society, indeed in order to function day to day, we must learn to understand and integrate these differences. The range of cultures we encounter in the multicultural cities in which we live may be slightly unusual, but only slightly, as migration patterns around the world respond to rapid economic and political changes. The world is becoming more interdependent; to keep pace we must all learn to think globally—we must all develop our *cultural intelligence!*

The aim of this book is to help you acquire the global people skills you need to deal with individuals from other cultural backgrounds, which will make you more effective in your all-around performance in the years ahead. It is for people who travel overseas and encounter new cultures, as well as for those who stay at home and find that other cultures have come to them. It is about acquiring the *cultural intelligence* not only to survive without embarrassment in a new multicultural environment but also to pursue your goals with the confidence needed for success.

Like its predecessors, this book is different from many other books you may have seen about cross-cultural skills or living and working in other countries.

First, this book is not country-specific. We do not provide laundry lists of drills and routines that should be applied in this country or that. Our intent is rather to help you to acquire a way of thinking and being that can be applied to any number of countries and cultures.

Second, this book is based on years of sound academic research. However, it is not an academic text, and we have tried to present important concepts in a straightforward way. To make the learning concrete, we have illustrated each chapter with a number of case studies in cross-cultural behavior, from various cultural settings.

Finally, we don't promise that this book will solve all your interpersonal problems, either at work or in your daily life. However, we sincerely believe that if you read and apply the concepts outlined here, you will be well on your way to acquiring a critical contemporary skill—cultural intelligence.

Cultural intelligence builds on earlier concepts that you have probably heard of: the intelligence quotient (IQ) and emotional intelligence (EQ), the idea that it is important how we handle our emotions. Cultural intelligence (CQ) incorporates the capability to interact effectively across cultures.

The concept is easy to understand, but it takes time and effort to develop high levels of skill. Becoming culturally intelligent is essentially learning by doing and has useful outcomes beyond the development of intercultural skills. In addition, different cultures are fascinating, and learning about them can be a lot of fun.

The first three chapters outline the fundamentals of cultural intelligence. Chapter 1 shows how a lack of cultural intelligence can negatively affect intercultural interactions. In it we examine the problems with current methods of addressing these cross-cultural issues and identify acquiring cultural intelligence as a more productive approach. The next two chapters outline the principles and practice of cultural intelligence. In Chapter 2 we help you to *understand* what cultural differences are and how they are reflected in different people's behavior. Chapter 3 helps you to *discard your assumptions* about the way people "should" behave, practice *mindfulness*—a kind of attention to culturally based behavior—and develop *skills* for use in cross-cultural situations. The message in these chapters is that the task of understanding culture is difficult but not impossible, and that if you learn the basic principles, adopt a mindful approach, and are prepared to act as a culturally adaptive person, you can function effectively in a variety of cross-cultural settings, and find the experience rewarding.

In the next four chapters we apply the fundamentals of cultural intelligence to a number of common interpersonal challenges in multicultural settings. By applying the principles outlined, you can be more effective in making decisions in different cultural contexts (Chapter 4); communicating, negotiating, and resolving conflicts across cultures (Chapter 5); leading and motivating others who are culturally different (Chapter 6); and designing, managing, and contributing to multicultural groups and teams (Chapter 7). In Chapter 8 you will learn how cross-cultural understanding, mindfulness, and skills are acquired and can be developed by means of education, everyday experience, and foreign travel. This edition also includes the newest measure of cultural intelligence, which is presented in the appendix. This measure is a result of a decade-long research project conducted by an international team of university-based researchers to define and measure the concept of cultural intelligence. The result is a short but theory-based measure of the concept that we hope will be a useful tool to assess and help individuals develop their cultural intelligence. Finally, we provide a bibliography of key sources for those wanting to explore cultural intelligence in more depth.

Kerr is a Scot who lives and works in New Zealand. Dave is a New Zealand citizen but was born and educated in the United States and now lives and works in Canada. As we write and teach about cultural diversity, we are constantly reminded of our own cultural backgrounds. While we both have extensive international experience and between us have lived and worked in eleven different countries, we know that these backgrounds influence how we think and write. We have worked very hard to be objective in this regard, but we would be pleased to hear from readers who feel we have missed or misinterpreted things that are obvious to them from their cultural perspective.

In this book we have attempted to help readers understand and integrate cultural differences, to appreciate the wonderful diversity of our fellow human beings all around the world, and to help people everywhere become more knowledgeable, more attentive, and more skilled in their interactions with others. We sincerely believe that by developing cultural intelligence, we can all make the world a more productive and a happier place.

Dave Thomas   *Kerr Inkson*
Vancouver   *Auckland*

Acknowledgments

Numerous individuals, organizations, and environments have contributed to the production of this volume. We are grateful to Berrett-Koehler for convincing us to make room in our schedules to do a third edition. We thank everyone at BK for caring about our books and making them the best they can be.

Many of the ideas in this book were the product of, or refined in, numerous discussions that Dave has had with members of the International Organization Network (ION). The development of this book was based on the work of the Cultural Intelligence Project. Led by Dave, the members of the original Cultural Intelligence Project are Kevin Au, Zeynep Aycan, Richard Brislin, Jean-Luc Cerdin, Bjørn Ekelund, Efrat Elron, Mila Lazarova, Martha Maznevski, Andre Pekerti, Steven Poelmans, Elizabeth Ravlin, and Günter Stahl. We are especially grateful to Stacey Fitzsimmons and Yuan Liao for their contributions to our work.

This volume is informed not only by our academic study but also by the numerous cross-cultural encounters that make culture come alive for us. Therefore, we thank all those people who have helped to educate us and beg forgiveness from those we have offended along the way through our own lack of cultural intelligence.

CHAPTER 1

Living and Working in the Global Village

I PROMISE TO TRY

Barbara Barnes, alone in her Minneapolis office, pounds her desk in frustration. She has just read an email from an irate customer, who complains that her department's technical representative, who has been visiting the customer to correct a fault in software supplied by Barbara's company, is not only unable to solve the problem but seems to have less knowledge of the software than the customer's own staff. The customer's business is being seriously disrupted. Can Barbara please send someone else, who knows what they are doing?

Worse, this is the third such incident reported to Barbara this week. It doesn't seem to be just a single employee fouling up—the whole technical department seems unable to resolve such issues. True, the software is new and initial bugs are to be expected. But Barbara recalls that several weeks ahead of the first delivery to customers, she had a conversation with Vijay, the section manager, who is on a two-year temporary assignment from the Delhi office. She had wanted Vijay's assurance that the technical staff would all be ready in time.

"Vijay," she said, "we have four weeks to get everyone up to scratch. There is still time to delay the launch, but it would cost customer goodwill. Can you do it in time?"

Vijay hesitated. "It will be difficult," he said. "Do you think it's possible?"

"I know it's tough," she said. "But if anyone can do it, you can."

Vijay smiled. "H'mmmm. In that case, we will do it."

"Thank you, Vijay."

He looked out of the window. "It's snowing again," he said. "I hate your winters. People get sick. Everything slows down."

Now, Barbara calls Vijay to her office and explains the problem to him.

"I thought you said all the technicians would be trained."

"Most of them have been. It is bad luck. There have been more technical issues and more staff sickness than we expected. But we can resolve this problem. I will reassign trained staff to the dissatisfied customers. And soon all the staff will be trained."

But Barbara can't stop the anger rising in her throat. "But Vijay," she said. "You *promised!*"

Vijay doesn't answer. He is too amazed to speak.

Did Vijay promise? Barbara is absolutely certain he did. Vijay is certain that he said only that he would try, and he pointed out the considerable difficulties. To understand the differences in perception, we have to understand cultural differences between home-grown Americans like Barbara and South Asians (Indians) like Vijay. The difference is about the *context* in which specific words—such as "we will do it"—are spoken. American culture stresses low-context communication; what matters is the precise meaning of the words spoken, regardless of context. In Vijay's high-context Indian culture, communication is heavily influenced by contextual cues, which in this case included Vijay's hesitation, his account of difficulties, and his reference to the weather. Another Indian overhearing the conversation would be clear that Vijay was promising to try but believed the task would be impossible.

Both Barbara and Vijay may have the best interests of their employer at heart, but the results of their miscommunication are potentially serious. The company has broken its trust with some of its customers. Just as Vijay is accountable to Barbara for the error, so will Barbara be accountable to her own boss for loss of customer goodwill. And, perhaps more seriously, both Barbara and Vijay may feel that they cannot trust the other again.

How did this happen? Barbara assumed too much from Vijay's words, failed to double-check the real meaning of his communication, and therefore did not hear Vijay's warning. Vijay likewise assumed he had made himself clear. These failures result from their lack of what we call *cultural intelligence*. If either of them had been able to understand and accommodate, at least in part, the other's culturally based customs and norms, and if they had tried harder to help each other to understand their own customs, they might have been able to check out each other's messages to ensure that they both understood the same thing.

The story of Barbara and Vijay is typical—it is a story that is enacted again and again, in different forms and in many situations around the world, as ordinary people grapple with the problem of relating to others who are from cultures where things are done differently.

Consider the following examples:

- A British company experiences inexplicable problems of morale and conflict with the workforce of its Japanese subsidiary. This seems out of character with the usual politeness and teamwork of the Japanese. Later it is found that the British manager of the operation in Japan is not taken seriously because she is a woman.

- Two American managers meet regularly with executives and engineers of a large Chinese electronics firm to present their idea for a joint venture. They notice that different engineers seem to be attending each meeting and that their questions are becoming more technical, making it difficult for the Americans to answer without giving away trade secrets. The Americans resent this attempt to gain technological information. Don't the Chinese have any business ethics? Later they learn that that such questioning is common practice and considered to be good business among the Chinese, who often suspect that Westerners are interested only in exploiting a cheap labor market.

- In Malaysia, an old woman struggles to unload furniture from a cart and carry it into her house. Many people crowd the street, but no one offers help. Two young American tourists who are passing see the problem, rush up, and start to help the old lady. The locals on the street seem bemused by these Americans helping someone they don't even know.

- A Canadian police superintendent's four key subordinates are, respectively, French-Canadian, East Indian, Chinese, and Persian. How can he deal with them equitably? How can he find a managerial style that works with all of them? Should he recognize their differences or treat them all the same?

- A Dutch couple, volunteering in Sri Lanka assisting local economic development, visit a Sri Lankan couple to whom they have been introduced. Their hosts are gracious and hospitable but very reserved. The guests feel awkward and find it hard to make conversation. Later, they worry about the ineptitude they felt in dealing with the Sri Lankans.

These stories provide real-life examples of people from different parts of the world struggling with problems caused by intercultural differences. Have you been in situations like the ones above that have left you puzzled and frustrated because you simply haven't felt tuned in to the people you have been dealing with? Do you wonder how to deal with people from other countries, cultures, or ethnic groups? If so, you are not alone; you are one of the many people attempting to operate in a new, multicultural world.

The Global Village

There are over seven billion people in the world, from many different cultures, yet we all live in a village where events taking place ten thousand miles away can seem as close as those on the next street. Whenever we read a newspaper or watch television or buy a product from the grocery store we find ourselves in this global village. We can watch a Middle East firefight as if we were there, eat tropical fruit with snow on the ground outside, and meet people from far-off places at the local mall. The following dramatic examples of globalization are familiar to almost everyone.

THE GLOBAL VILLAGE BECOMES APPARENT

In the new millennium, Westerners' consciousness of the increasingly global society that they live in has been powerfully raised by various major crises.

On September 11, 2001, the world came to America in a new and horrifying way. The young men who flew their hijacked airliners into the great U.S. citadels of the World Trade Center and the Pentagon were citizens of the global village. They were operating in a world with a profoundly increased consciousness of difference—haves versus have-nots, Christians versus Muslims—as well as far fewer boundaries. To the terrorists, America was not a distant vision but an outrage beamed nightly into their homes through their televisions, yet only a plane-trip away. They slipped easily into the world's most powerful nation, acquired its language, and took flying lessons from friendly, helpful locals.

The news of the attacks traveled, virtually instantaneously, to all corners of the world. Californians stared aghast at the strange horrors of the day's breakfast show. Europeans crowded around television screens in appliance store windows. Australians phoned each other in the night and said, "Switch your telly on." A billion viewers around the globe watched as the Twin Towers collapsed in front of their eyes.

In October 2008 people around the world again watched in horror as the morass labeled GFC (global financial crisis) spread quickly into their lives. Some of the biggest and apparently most impregnable financial institutions suddenly went out of business, crippled by multibillion-dollar debts. Flows of credit—the lifeblood of business—froze, and stock markets plunged. Firms closed down and staff was laid off. Political leaders struggled to resolve the issue by freeing up trillions of dollars for bailouts of stricken banks—a de facto reversal of their most cherished principles of free-market capitalism. Yet it was only when the world's leaders *all* came together in meetings of the leading industrialized counties and developed integrated *global* solutions to a global problem, that the bleeding stopped and markets around the world began to stabilize. Even so, it is only now, in 2017, that many countries are beginning to put the global financial crisis behind them.

In September 2015 the photo of Aylan Kurdi, a three-year-old Syrian boy who had drowned and washed up on a beach in Turkey, shocked the world. He and his family were part of the most significant refugee crisis since the Second World War. His mother, Rehan, and five-year-old brother, Galip, also perished. Only his father Abdullah survived the perilous sea journey. The photo of Aylan brought the plight of Syria's millions of refugees to world attention. Other refugees fled to Europe from conflicts in Libya, Afghanistan, and other countries. Despite the efforts of many governments and aid agencies, as 2015 drew to a close, the world had yet to come to grips with this massive migration. As the world's great countries squabbled about how many each could absorb, four million refugees were registered and camped around Europe. The problems of integrating them will be massive, and they will not be only economic and political problems but also *cultural.*

After these events, people said, "The world will never be the same again." They might rather have said: "The world has been changing rapidly for some time. These events have caused us to notice it."

Such events are not just about America or Europe and the Middle East; they are *global.* Economic, political, legal, and cultural forces are at work that cross international boundaries, create international problems, and require international solutions. We are all involved, all of us citizens in a global world. None of us can escape that.

Forces of Globalization

As we increasingly live global lives, we are beginning to understand the importance of globalization, particularly its effects on our lives. Globalization increases the permeability of traditional boundaries, not just those around organizations but those around countries, economies, industries, and people.[1]

Globalization has been accelerated by many factors, including the following:

- Increased international interconnectedness, represented by the growth of international trade and trade agreements, multinational corporations, and the relocation of businesses wherever cost is lowest.

- The increased migration, both legal and illegal, particularly from less-developed to more-developed countries. In virtually every nation are many people who were born and brought up in other countries or are culturally influenced by their immigrant families.

- The ability of information and communication technology to transcend time and distance so that at the touch of a computer keyboard or a mobile phone, we can be somewhere else, thousands of kilometers away, participating in events and changing outcomes there.

Until recently, only a few very large multinational organizations were concerned with foreign operations. Now even very small organizations may be global; indeed, small and medium-sized organizations, which increasingly can survive only if they export their products, account for a growing share of global business.

Because of globalization, the environment of organizations is now more complex, more dynamic, more uncertain, and more competitive than ever before. These trends are unlikely to reverse or decrease. Tomorrow's managers, even more than today's, must learn to compete and work in a global world.

Globalization of People

Globalization affects managers, employees at all levels, customers, and indeed everyone! It brings about interactions and relationships between people who are culturally different. As organizational members, as tourists, and as members of networks and communities that have "gone international," we travel overseas among people from other cultures, telephone or Skype them, correspond with them by e-mail, and befriend them on Facebook. Even in our home cities, more and more of our colleagues, clients, and even the people we pass in the street are from cultures that are different from our own.

This globalization of culturally different people creates a major challenge. Unlike legal, political, or economic aspects of the global environment, which are observable, culture is largely invisible and is therefore the aspect of the global context that is most often overlooked.

The potential problems are enormous. Even people from the same culture often lack interpersonal skills. When interpersonal interaction takes place across cultural boundaries, the potential for misunderstanding and failure is compounded.

The conclusion is clear. You are a member of the global community, even if you are not conscious of it and even if you have never done business abroad or even traveled abroad. You may never have gone around the globe, but the globe has come to you. Any organization you work for will most likely buy or sell in another country, or will be influenced by global events. You will increasingly have to interact with people from all parts of the globe.

Here is a story about two global people. One is an international migrant who is trying to find a new life in a very different place. The other is a manager who has never left her own country.

THE JOB APPLICANT

In California, a human-resources manager sits in her office. She is interviewing candidates for factory work. Suddenly a dark-skinned young man walks in without knocking. He does not look at the manager but walks to the nearest chair and, without waiting to be invited, sits down. He looks down at the floor. The manager is appalled at such graceless behavior. The interview has not even started, and even though the jobs being filled do not require social skills, the young man is already unlikely to be appointed.

Observing this scene, most Americans and Western Europeans would understand why the manager felt as she did. The man's behavior certainly seems odd and disrespectful.

But suppose we tell the manager more about the young man. He was born and brought up in Samoa and only recently immigrated to the United States. Samoans have great respect for authority, and the young man sees the manager as an authority figure deserving of respect. In Samoa you do not speak to, or even make eye contact with, authority figures until they invite you to do so. You do not stand while they are sitting, because to do so would put you on a physically higher level than they are, implying serious disrespect. In other words, according to the norms of his own cultural background, the young man has behaved exactly as he should. The human resource manager, based on her own culture, expects him to greet her politely, make eye contact, offer a handshake, and wait to be invited to sit down. In doing so, she is being unfair not only to candidates who operate differently, she is also reducing her company's opportunity to benefit from people with other cultural backgrounds. As an employer of Samoans and other ethnic and cultural minorities, she would benefit from exposure to Samoan customs and training in cross-cultural communication. Of course, if the company employs the man, he may have to learn appropriate ways of interacting with Westerners. Both would benefit from reading this book!

We are all different, yet we often expect everyone else to be like us. If they don't do things the way we would do them, we assume there is something wrong with them. Why can't we think outside our little cultural rulebooks, accept and enjoy the wonderful diversity of humankind, and learn to work in harmony with others' ways?

The characters in the cases we have provided so far—Barbara, Vijay, the human-resources manager, and the young Samoan man—are all, perhaps inadvertently, playing a game called *Be Like Me*. Do it *my* way. Follow *my* rules. We all tend to play Be Like Me with the people we live and work with. And, when the other party can't, or doesn't want to be like us, we—as do the characters in these cases—withdraw into baffled incomprehension.

Intercultural Failures

Many of us fail in intercultural situations in all sorts of ways, such as the following:

- Being unaware of the key features and biases of our own culture. Just as other cultures may seem odd to us, ours may be odd to people from other cultures. For example, few Americans realize how noisy their natural extroversion and assertive conversation seem to those whose cultures value reticence and modesty. Similarly, people from Asian societies, where long silences in conversations are considered normal, do not realize how odd and intimidating silence may seem to Westerners.

- Feeling threatened or uneasy when interacting with people who are culturally different. We may try hard not to be prejudiced against them, but we notice, usually with tiny internal feelings of apprehension, the physical characteristics that differentiate them from us.

- Being unable to understand or explain the behavior of others who are culturally different. What motivates us is often very different from what motivates the behavior of people from other cultures. Trying to explain their behavior in terms of our own motives is often a mistake.

- Failing to apply knowledge about one culture to a different culture. Even people who travel internationally all the time are unable to use this experience to be more effective in subsequent intercultural encounters.

- Not recognizing the influence of our own cultural background. Culture programs our behavior at a very deep level of consciousness. Behavior that is normal to us may seem abnormal or even bizarre to people from other cultures.

- Being unable to adjust to living and working in another culture. Anyone who has lived in a foreign culture can attest to this difficulty. The severity of culture shock may vary, but it affects us all.

- Being unable to develop long-term interpersonal relationships with people from other cultures. Even if we learn how to understand them and communicate with them a little better, the effort of doing so puts us off trying to develop the relationship any further.

In all of these examples, stress and anxiety are increased for all parties, and the end result is often impaired performance, less satisfaction and personal growth, and lost opportunities for our organizations.

Ways of Overcoming Cultural Differences

If these are the symptoms, what is the cure? How can we ordinary people feel at home when dealing with those from other cultures? How can we know what to say and do? How can we pursue business and other relationships with the same relaxation and synergy that we experience in relationships with people from our own culture?

One way of trying to deal with the problem is to stick to the *Be Like Me* policy and try to brazen it out. If we come from a dominant economy or culture such as the United States, we can reason that it is for us to set norms and for others to imitate us.

You may think there is something in this. First, a dominant culture may win in the end anyway.[2] For example, the English language is becoming the lingua franca of global business and education, and it is increasingly spoken in business and professional interactions all over Europe and in large parts of Asia. Second, many people believe that different cultures are converging to a common norm, assisted by phenomena such as mass communication and the "McDonaldization" of consumption.[3] Eventually, they argue, the whole world will become like the United States anyway, and its citizens will think, talk, and act like Americans. Many cities around the world already mimic New York, with the same organizations, brands, architectural and dress styles: why resist the process?

In fact, the evidence in favor of cultural convergence is not compelling. Convergence is probably taking place only in superficial matters such as business procedures and some consumer preferences.[4] Also, such convergence robs us of the great gift of diversity and the novel ways of thinking and working that it brings.

UNDERSTANDING CULTURAL DIFFERENCES

Can we solve the problem of cultural differences and seize the opportunity they create simply by learning what other cultures are like? Do we even know, in any organized way, what they are like?

Information about other cultures is easily accessible. Cultural anthropologists have researched many of the cultures of the world and cultural differences affecting specific fields, such as education, health, and business, have also been explored.[5] This information has been useful in establishing the behavior or cultural stereotypes of many national cultures, and provides a starting point for anticipating culturally based behavior. Understanding cultural differences between countries and how those differences affect behavior is a first step toward gaining cultural intelligence. This book provides some basic information on these matters.

However, this basic knowledge is only the beginning of the process of changing cultural differences from a handicap to an asset. Even at their best, experts on cultural difference, who say things such as "Japanese behave in this way and Americans in that" can provide only broad generalizations, which often conceal huge variances and considerable subtlety. A country may have, for example, religious or tribal or ethnic or regional differences, or forms of special protocol.

The *laundry-list* approach to cross-cultural understanding attempts to provide each individual with a list—"everything you need to know"—about a particular country. Such lists often attempt to detail not only a country's key cultural characteristics but also regional variations, customs to be followed, speech inflections to use, expressions and actions that might be considered offensive, and functional information on matters such as living costs, health services, and education. Tourists and travelers can buy books of this type about most countries, and some companies take this approach to preparing employees and their families for foreign assignments.

Laundry lists have their place, but they are cumbersome. They have to document every conceivable cultural variation, along with drills and routines to cater for them. For an expatriate, this intensive preparation for a single destination may be appropriate, but for most of us, our engagement with other cultures involves a less intensive interaction with a variety of cultures. If we travel to half a dozen countries, entertain visitors from a variety of places abroad, or interact with a large range of immigrants, must we learn an elaborate laundry list for each culture? If we are introduced to culturally different people without warning and have no laundry list readily available, how can we cope? Even in our own country we may be introduced to a new co-worker whose culture we haven't encountered before.

Furthermore, laundry lists tend to be dry and formal. The essence of culture is subtler, is expressed in combination with the unique personality of each individual, and is hard to state in print. Formal and abstract knowledge needs to be supplemented by, and integrated with, experience of the culture and interactions with its people. Learning facts is not enough.

BECOMING CULTURALLY INTELLIGENT

A third approach to the problem is to become culturally intelligent.[6]

Cultural intelligence means being skilled and flexible about understanding a culture, interacting with it to learn more about it, reshaping your thinking to have more empathy for it, and becoming more skilled when interacting with others from it. We must become flexible and able to adapt to each new cultural situation with knowledge and sensitivity.

Cultural intelligence consists of three parts.

- First, the culturally intelligent person requires knowledge of what culture is, how cultures vary, and how culture affects behavior.

- Second, the culturally intelligent person needs to practice mindfulness, the ability to pay attention reflectively and creatively to cues in the situations encountered and to one's own knowledge and feelings.

- Third, based on knowledge and mindfulness, the culturally intelligent person develops cross-cultural skills and becomes competent across a range of situations, choosing the appropriate behavior from a repertoire of behaviors that are correct for a range of intercultural situations.

The model in Figure 1.1 is a graphic representation of cultural intelligence.

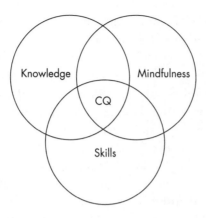

FIGURE 1.1. Components of cultural intelligence (CQ)

Each element in Figure 1.1 is interrelated with the others. The process of becoming culturally intelligent involves a cycle or repetition in which each new challenge builds upon previous ones. This approach has the advantage over the laundry-list method that, as well as acquiring competence in a specific culture, you simultaneously acquire *general* cultural intelligence, making each new challenge easier to face.

You have probably heard of the psychologists' concept of intelligence and its measure, the intelligence quotient (IQ). More recently has come recognition of emotional intelligence, the ability to handle our emotions, and its measure, the emotional intelligence quotient (EQ). Cultural intelligence (or CQ) describes and assesses the capability to interact effectively across cultures.[7]

In the chapters that follow, we present a road map for developing your cultural intelligence by addressing its three elements one by one.

In Chapter 2 we examine the necessary information base, which includes a secure *knowledge* of what culture is and is not; its depth, strength, and systematic nature; and some of the main types of cultural differences. This provides a good basic set of tools to give one confidence in any cross-cultural situation.

In Chapter 3 we consider how observation of the everyday behavior of people from different backgrounds can be useful in interpreting the knowledge introduced in Chapter 2. Most people operate interpersonally in "cruise control," interpreting their experiences from the standpoint of their own culture. We develop the idea of *mindfulness*[8]—a process of observing and reflecting on cross-cultural knowledge. Developing mindfulness is a key means of improving cultural intelligence. We then outline how knowledge and mindfulness lead to new *skilled behavior.* By developing a new repertoire of behaviors, you can translate the understanding of culture into effective cross-cultural interactions.

Cultural intelligence is not difficult to understand but is hard to learn and to put into practice on an ongoing basis. It takes time and effort to develop a high CQ. Years of studying, observing, reflecting, and experimenting may lie ahead before one develops truly skilled performance. Because becoming culturally intelligent is substantially learning by doing, it has useful outcomes beyond the development of intercultural skills. In addition, new cultures are intriguing: learning how to live or work in them or to interact with their people can be fun, with possibilities of new insights, new relationships, and a new richness in your life. This book is the place to start on this journey.

Summary

This chapter describes the forces of globalization that are dramatically changing the environment not just for global managers but for everyone. We are all becoming global participants in our organizations; even those who stay in their own countries have to think in global terms. The essence of being global is interacting with people who are culturally different. Culture is more difficult to deal with than other aspects of the environment because much of how culture operates is invisible. Although we know much about cultures around the world, this knowledge is only the starting point to becoming culturally intelligent. Cultural intelligence involves understanding the fundamentals of intercultural interaction, developing a mindful approach to them, and building a repertoire of cross-cultural behaviors suited to different intercultural situations. For everyone living and working in today's global environment, interacting effectively across cultures is now a fundamental requirement.

CHAPTER 2

Cultural Knowledge

Chan Yuk Fai ushered his British guest into the crowded Shanghai restaurant. Around them, the atmosphere was busy with the quiet babble of a dozen conversations. Mr. Chan bowed slightly, then leaned forward and smiled. "I think," he said in excellent English, "I think the food is not the very best in this restaurant."

Jeffrey Thomson stiffened slightly. He found it hard to conceal his surprise. What was he to make of Mr. Chan's remark? Mr. Chan had chosen the restaurant. Did he really think the food was poor? If he thought so, why had he chosen this restaurant? Perhaps criticizing the food was just a Chinese custom—something everyone did that had nothing to do with the real quality of the food. Perhaps it was a joke—Mr. Chan was smiling broadly. After all, what did Jeffrey know about the Chinese sense of humor? Or perhaps it was an affectation of modesty. He had read somewhere that Chinese were self-effacing. But he had also read that they were indirect. Maybe criticizing the restaurant was Mr. Chan's way of saying he did not have a lot of interest in Jeffrey or what he had to say. Maybe it was even some form of veiled insult!

He realized that Mr. Chan was politely waiting for him to respond and that he had no idea what to say. He felt very confused.

Best to be noncommittal, he thought. What would I say if someone said that to me in London? He smiled back at Mr. Chan. "I'm sure we can make the best of it," he replied.

Was it his imagination, or did he see a minuscule reduction in Mr. Chan's beaming smile?[1]

On the surface Jeffrey Thomson's worries about Chinese culture are about Chinese customs, the ways in which people habitually go about day-to-day activities. The Chinese custom is to show respect for a guest by disparaging one's own accomplishments, even the selection of a restaurant. Chinese people expect that the guest will return this respect with a compliment. By not doing so, Jeffrey has made a cultural blunder. This custom is specific to the cultural situation, but Jeffrey's predicament is one that thousands of other travelers from all continents and countries experience. Jeffrey *does* have some understanding of the cultural differences that exist between himself and Mr. Chan, including his reflection that Chinese people tend to be self-effacing and inscrutable. And he is looking for clues to help him to draw the right conclusion and behave correctly. But his knowledge, his insight, and his experience are simply insufficient for the task. He lacks cultural intelligence.

Components of Cultural Intelligence

Jeffrey's problem can be divided into three linked components.

First, he lacks detailed *knowledge*. He understands that cross-cultural differences exist. He has remembered a few characteristics of Chinese people. But these are crude stereotypes, of little help in enabling him to understand the situation.

Second, he lacks *mindfulness*. Not only does he not know what Mr. Chan's remark means, but he lacks the ability to observe and interpret the remark in the context of other cues—prior conversations, his dealings with other Chinese, the visible quality of the restaurant, Mr. Chan's smile, and so on. Because of this, he is unable to read the situation as it develops. Whatever the outcome, he is likely to learn little from the experience. Mindfulness is a means of continually observing and understanding cultural meanings, and using that understanding for immediate action and long-term learning.

Third, he lacks the *skill* to adapt his behavior. He would love to be able to respond confidently and authentically but also sensitively to his host. He realizes that being able to respond appropriately would put both himself and Mr. Chan at ease and would help their conversation. But because of his lack of both knowledge and interpretive skill the only action he is capable of is to respond as he would "at home." Jeffrey needs to develop a repertoire of behaviors that will enable him to act appropriately in any cross-cultural situation.

The three components combine to provide intercultural flexibility and competence. In brief, culturally intelligent people have

- the *knowledge* to understand cross-cultural phenomena
- the *mindfulness* to observe and interpret particular situations
- the *skills* required to adapt *behavior* to act appropriately in a range of situation

These three components are interconnected and build on each other. Because culturally intelligent people have good background understanding, their interpretation is assisted— they know what to look for. But each competency is also based on wider personal characteristics. The people who find cultural intelligence easiest to acquire are interested in novel learning and social interaction and have good communication skills. But those who are unsure of themselves in these areas will likely find that acquiring cultural intelligence increases their competence and confidence in *all* interpersonal situations.[2]

In this chapter we focus on the information base—or *knowledge*—that is the first component of cultural intelligence. Here, what is needed is a basic understanding of culture.

What Culture Is

The word *culture* is familiar to everyone, but what exactly does it mean? A useful definition by noted social scientist Geert Hofstede is that culture consists of shared mental programs that condition individuals' responses to their environment.[3] Thus, culture is inherent in everyday behavior, such as Chan Yuk Fai's and Jeffrey Thomson's efforts at conversation, but such behavior is controlled by deeply embedded mental programs. Culture is not just a set of surface behaviors; it is deeply entrenched in each of us. The surface features of our social behavior—for example, our mannerisms, our ways of speaking to each other, the way we dress—are often manifestations of deep culturally based values and principles.

A key feature of culture is that these mental programs are *shared*—Chan Yuk Fai and Jeffrey Thomson share theirs with many other people from their own ethnic or national communities. Hofstede talks about three levels of mental programming, as shown in Figure 2.1.

- The deepest level—human nature—is based on common biological reactions, such as hunger, sex drive, territoriality, and nurturing of the young, that all members of the human race have in common, even though they come from different cultures.

- The shallowest level—personality—is based on the specific genetic makeup and personal experiences that make each individual unique. For example, we may be sociable or introverted, aggressive or submissive, emotional or stable, or perhaps, as a result of learning, have a deep interest in fashionable clothing or a love of good wine.

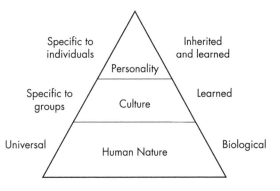

FIGURE 2.1. Three levels of mental programming

Because of personality, each of us has many characteristics that are different from those of others, even though they come from the same culture.

- The middle level—culture—is based on common experiences that we share with a particular group: values, attitudes, and assumptions about proper behavior that we have in common with the group, but not with those outside the group. The group may be large, such as a national population, for example Japanese culture; or small, for example the culture of the committee of a local PTA. In recent years, many business, government, and not-for-profit organizations have recognized the power of culture to shape individual values and actions and have worked hard to establish "organization cultures" that will bond the activities of diverse members to common values and themes such as customer service or conservation.[4]

In this book, we are concerned mostly with national or ethnic cultures. But the notion of smaller cultures—sometimes referred to as subcultures—and the idea of individual personality remind us that huge variation exists within any given culture and that one of the biggest barriers to effective intercultural interaction is basing our behavior on stereotypes, which assume that all members of a given cultural group are identical.

Characteristics of Culture

Culture has some basic characteristics that are worth keeping in mind.

CULTURE IS SHARED

By definition, culture is something that a group has in common that is not normally available to people outside the group. It is mental programming held in common that enables insiders to interact with each other with a special intimacy denied to outsiders.

For example, Scottish people all over the world share an understanding of history that is rooted in conflict with, and oppression by, the English. Even though the two groups nowadays coexist relatively harmoniously, this simple fact creates a bond among Scots and an attitude toward the English that is hard to put into words but is immediately recognized by Scottish people when they meet anywhere in the world.

CULTURE IS LEARNED AND IS ENDURING

The example of the Scots and the English tells us that culture does not arise by accident but builds up systematically over time based on sequences of historical events. The mental programming of a group is learned by its members over long periods as they interact with their environment and with each other. Some aspects of culture, such as religious beliefs, systems of land ownership, and forms of marriage, are built into institutions. Other aspects are passed on through the stories that parents tell their children and through the role models they provide.

CULTURE IS A POWERFUL INFLUENCE ON BEHAVIOR

We have a hard time escaping our culture, even when we want to. The mental programming involved is strong. Even when we question the rationality of some aspects of our culture or seek to adopt cultural flexibility by doing things in line with a different culture, we have a natural tendency to revert to our cultural roots.

For example, one young man was brought up in a strict Christian culture that taught him that the theater is the house of the devil. When he went to university and mixed with more liberal people, he decided that from a rational point of view there was nothing wrong with going to the theater. But on his first visit, he became nauseous and had to leave to be sick. His culture had programmed him extremely powerfully. To some extent this book, in encouraging cultural flexibility in cross-cultural situations, is asking readers to try to do something that may not come naturally.

Nevertheless, the experience of migrants, who deliberately and often successfully move from one cultural setting to another, suggests that individuals can learn, and even identify with, aspects of a new culture. In some cases, the requirements of a dominant culture may even cause them to suppress aspects of their original culture. These changes take place through a process known as acculturation.[5] Being embedded in an unfamiliar setting causes some to learn actively about the new culture, while others attempt to avoid it, often by trying to re-create their old culture in the new situation.[6] The best adaptation is done by those who learn the new culture while still retaining valuable elements of their original culture. By so doing, they cultivate cultural intelligence.[7]

CULTURE IS SYSTEMATIC AND ORGANIZED

Culture is not random. It is an organized system of values, attitudes, beliefs, and meanings that are related to each other and to the context. When Chan Yuk Fai says, "I think the food is not the very best in this restaurant," understanding that Chinese people often deprecate themselves is not enough. We need to understand that such deprecation is but one tiny expression of a complex system of values and ideas. It is a surface representation of Mr. Chan's deepest values and understanding of the world—a mental program based on centuries of survival and cooperation by Mr. Chan's Chinese ancestors in their largely agricultural economy and culture. As another example, the practice of polygamy, which is frowned on in most cultures, makes good historical sense in some African cultures where it is still practiced. Acceptance of polygamy depends on such factors as family status, economic security, and religious commitment, all of which are based on having more children, and particularly more sons, per family.

Because of the mental programming imposed by our own culture, the cultures of other people often seem strange and illogical. Deeper scrutiny can reveal that each culture has its own, often exquisite, logic and coherence.

CULTURE IS LARGELY INVISIBLE

What we see of culture is expressed in living artifacts, which include communicated messages such as that of Mr. Chan concerning the food. But they also include human activities such as language, customs, and dress, as well as physical artifacts such as architecture, art, and decoration.

Because much of culture is hidden, these obvious and visible elements of culture may be likened to the tip of an iceberg.[8] Icebergs have as much as 90 percent of their mass below the surface of the water, leaving only a small percentage visible. The important part of the iceberg that is culture is not the obvious physical symbols that are above the surface but the deep underlying values and assumptions that they express. So understanding cultures involves a lot more than just understanding immediate surface behavior such as bows, handshakes, invitations, ceremonies, and body language. The invisible elements of culture—the underlying values, social structures, and ways of thinking—are the most important.

CULTURE MAY BE "TIGHT" OR "LOOSE"

Cultures differ from each other not just in their details but also in their pervasiveness.[9] Some societies are characterized by almost 100 percent agreement as to the form of correct behavior; other societies may have greater diversity and tolerance of difference. "Tight" cultures have uniformity and agreement and are often based on homogeneous populations or the dominance of particular religious beliefs. Japan is a good example. Countries such as Canada with diverse populations have relatively "loose" cultures, which in some cases are made even looser by the encouragement of freedom of thought and action.

National and Global Culture

As we have mentioned, nation and culture are not identical. Many ethnic cultures, organization cultures, minority cultures, and subcultures may influence different people within the same country. For example, the indigenous peoples of North America have cultural characteristics very different from those of the majority of Canadians and Americans, and both the United States and Canada have many distinctive cultural groupings within their populations. The main focus of this book, however, is on national culture.

Nations are often formed because of cultural similarities among different population groups, and over time they reinforce their adherence to a national culture by means of shared institutions, legal and educational systems, and, of course, nowadays, the mass media. National cultures are particularly important in international business because of the concept of national sovereignty and the need to conduct business affairs within a nation's legal and political frameworks.

Another issue relating to national culture concerns the

apparent growth of "global culture." Some people argue that as travel, business, and the media become more international, all countries converge toward a single culture, ironing out all the special differences that make each national culture unique. Because of the economic dominance of Western countries, particularly the United States and the larger European democracies, some people think that these countries' cultural forms will gradually submerge other cultures around the world. Thus, the international proliferation of organizations such as McDonald's and Starbucks is often welcomed as a sign of economic success, while also being criticized as an intrusion of American culture.

If the convergence theory were correct, it might be a reason to downplay the notion of cultural intelligence. If this were the case, it could be best to work with people from all nations to help them to get away from their own cultural habits and instead to understand and practice values and customs that are becoming standard around the world.

We think that this is a bad strategy for several reasons:

1. While some evidence supports the convergence theory, other evidence opposes it.[10] Many cultures may be becoming "modern," but they are doing so in different ways. Cultures tend to accept some aspects of other societies and reject others. In Hong Kong, for example, people have retained their traditional Chinese respect for authority while rejecting its fatalism, and have adopted modern competitiveness but rejected modern attitudes toward sexual freedom. Across the world, probably the only real convergence that is taking place is in surface matters such as basic business structures and consumer preferences, rather than in fundamental ways of thinking and behaving.

2. A society may also appear to accept change, but in fact the change is often recontextualized to fit preexisting cultural patterns.[11] For example, even though a McDonald's restaurant may look very much the same in any part of

the world, the experience of visiting a McDonald's is very different for Japanese or Chinese or French or U.S. people. For example, people from many Western countries see McDonald's as the place one goes to for fast food, but many Chinese people visit McDonald's to have an "American experience."

3. Even if convergence is taking place, the pace of change is very slow. The evolution of culture in any society is not easily predicted.[12] Traditional cultural patterns tend to be deeply embedded. Those who intend to sit back and wait for the rest of the world to catch up with the West in terms of culture will have to wait for a very long time.

4. Societies worldwide are recognizing the value of diversity in human affairs. Just as biodiversity has a value in allowing ecosystems to deal with major change, so too does cultural diversity offer us a wider range of viewpoints and ways of doing things. Many societies nowadays go out of their way to ensure that cultures under threat are protected from submergence by majority cultures.

Key Cultural Values

In Chapter 1, we rejected the laundry-list approach to understanding cultures—learning everything one needs to know about every culture one is likely to deal with—on the basis that cultures are so diverse and so complex that the task is impossible.

Nevertheless, we can "unpackage" cultures by describing their essential features to aid understanding. It is a bit like the language we use to describe people. Sally may be a unique individual with specific qualities and quirks of character that would take a long time to describe. But if we say Sally is intelligent, extroverted, emotionally stable, and unassertive, we have in a few words conveyed a lot of information that might differentiate Sally from other people.

Just as we can summarize people's individual character-istics, we can summarize the characteristics of a culture. An important way to describe both the similarities and differ-ences among cultures is by their underlying values. These cultural values are fundamental shared beliefs about how things should be or how one should behave.

Consider the following case.

careers. They have difficulty in understanding each other. "How can you let yourself be so dependent on others?" says Barry. "Some people would see it as nepotistic and corrupt." "How can you live your life as a man apart?" says Miguel. "Don't you care about the people who help you? Some people would see you as selfish and ungrateful."

The explanation for the cross-cultural misunderstanding in the case of Barry and Miguel is based on an important dimension of variation between cultures. Latin Americans have a much more group-oriented culture than Americans. Many activities, ranging from the kind of job seeking referred to above to methods of decision making, are based on groups—extended families, organization departments, volunteer groups. This results because of differentiating factors called *individualism* and *collectivism*.

- In *individualist* cultures people are most concerned about the consequences of action for themselves, not others. They prefer activities conducted on one's own or in relatively private interactions with friends. Decisions are made by the individual according to his or her own judgment as to what is appropriate and on the individual rewards that will accrue.

- In *collectivist* cultures, people primarily view themselves as members of groups and collectives rather than as autonomous individuals. They are concerned about the effects of actions on these groups and the approval of other people in their groups. Their activities are more likely to be undertaken in groups on a more public basis. Decisions are made on a consensual or consultative basis, and the effects of the decision on everyone in the social group are taken into account.

Individualism and collectivism are not either/or. They are values dimensions along which different cultures can be understood. Of all measures of cultural variation, individualism and collectivism may be the most useful and powerful.[13] However, it is important not to simplify these dimensions by, for example, equating individualism with selfishness or introversion, or collectivism with socialism. Both individualists and collectivists have relationships and groups, but the type of relationship is different: collectivists actually tend to have fewer groups with which they identify, but these are wide, diverse groups, such as tribes or extended families, and the bonds of loyalty are strong. Individualists often identify with many different groups, but the bonds are superficial. Individualism is most common in developed Western countries. A strong relationship exists between a country's individualism and its wealth (Gross National Product, or GNP).[14] The recent political fashion of free markets and the encouragement of entrepreneurship play to individualism, and developed countries have seen a marked international trend in this direction, leading, for example, to a general decline in individuals' loyalty to their employing organizations, and, indeed, their organizations' loyalty to them. Individualism and collectivism provide a basis for describing national culture in terms of the country's position on these dimensions and for comparing any two national cultures on the same basis. When other dimensions or aspects of culture are added to the picture, more detailed assessments and comparisons can be made.

SCHWARTZ VALUE SURVEY

Individualism and collectivism, while perhaps the most important dimensions of cultural variation, are not the only dimensions that researchers have been able to identify. For example, Israeli psychologist Shalom Schwartz and his colleagues did a more recent and more sophisticated mapping of cultures according to their value orientations.[15] They identified three universal requirements that every culture has: the need to specify how individuals should relate to the wider society, the need for society to preserve itself, and the need to define how society should relate to the natural world. Schwartz's idea was that while all societies have to address these requirements, they do so in different ways. In each society this leads to a shared set of fundamental beliefs about how things should be or how one should behave. By examining fifty-seven national cultures, Schwartz and colleagues derived seven fundamental value dimensions:

- Egalitarianism—recognition of people as moral equals
- Harmony—fitting in harmoniously with the environment
- Embeddedness—people as part of a collective
- Hierarchy—unequal distribution of power
- Mastery—exploitation of the natural or social environment
- Affective autonomy—pursuit of positive experiences
- Intellectual autonomy—independent pursuit of one's own ideas

Figure 2.2 shows the relative positions of countries along the seven dimensions.

It is impossible to represent perfectly the relative position of countries on seven dimensions in the two-dimensional space of the printed page. However, by using a technique called a co-plot, Schwartz and his colleagues were able to present the relationships quite accurately. The position of each country along the vector of each cultural dimension indicates how similar or different each country is on that dimension. For example, Canada and New Zealand are very similar on all seven dimensions. However, the United States, which is similar to these two countries on other dimensions, ranks higher on the mastery dimension (more like Japan). By examining the position of your own country and that of others on this map you can increase your knowledge about the

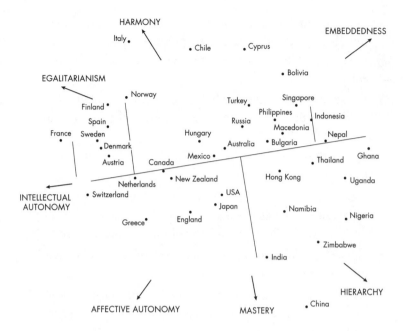

FIGURE 2.2. Co-plot of value dimensions across national cultures
Source: Adapted from Sagiv & Schwartz (2000)

areas of potential cultural harmony or conflict with members of another culture.

THE GLOBE STUDY

Another way of understanding similarities and differences across cultures is to examine which countries cluster together in their positions on various measures of cultural values. Based on a large-scale study of cultural differences in values, researchers who conducted the Global Leadership and Organizational Behavior Effectiveness (GLOBE) study grouped the sixty-two societies they studied into ten clusters.[16] These clusters, shown in Figure 2.3, are based on overall similarity of countries based on nine value orientations.

Cultural Knowledge   33

- *Institutional Collectivism:* The degree to which organizational and societal institutional practices encourage and reward collective distribution of resources and collective action

- *In-Group Collectivism:* The degree to which individuals express pride, loyalty, and cohesiveness in their organizations or families

- *Power Distance:* The degree to which members of a collective expect power to be distributed unequally

- *Uncertainty Avoidance:* The extent to which a society, organization, or group relies on social norms, rules, and procedures to alleviate unpredictability of future events

- *Gender Egalitarianism:* The degree to which a collective minimizes gender inequality

- *Assertiveness:* The degree to which individuals are assertive, confrontational, and aggressive in their relationships with others

- *Humane Orientation:* The degree to which a collective rewards individuals for being fair, altruistic, generous, caring, and kind to others

- *Future Orientation:* The extent to which individuals engage in future-oriented behaviors such as delayed gratification, planning, and investing in the future

- *Performance Orientation:* The degree to which a collective encourages and rewards group members for performance improvement and excellence

As shown in Figure 2.3, the clusters of countries reflect such factors as common language, common religion, common climate, geographic proximity, common economic system, and shared political boundaries—all of which can be shown to contribute to national cultural variation.[17] This typology underscores the historical basis of cultural variation. For example, the composition of the Anglo cluster indicates

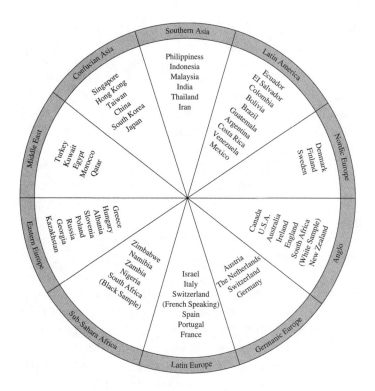

FIGURE 2.3. Country clusters according to the GLOBE study

that as a result of migration this culture was diffused from England to Ireland, the United States, Canada, South Africa, Australia, and New Zealand, and its position relative to other clusters indicates its own roots in Saxony (Germany) and Jutland (northern Denmark). Likewise the Confucian Asian cultural cluster reflects the strong historical influence of China and Confucian ideology. Even physically isolated Japan shared significant cultural interactions with China over time. As with the mapping of the Schwartz value orientations, by referring to the GLOBE cultural clusters you can get a first approximation of the extent to which you might share cultural values with people from other societies.

Effects of Culture: The "In-Group" and the "Out-Group"

An important aspect of culture is the way we use it to define ourselves. If we state that we are "American," "Thai," "Muslim," or that we "work for IBM," our assertion places us inside a boundary that excludes a lot of other people. It differentiates us. It sets up expectations—intentional or unintentional—as to the kinds of attitudes and behavior that others can expect from us.

This tendency is important in terms of bias—typically bias is in favor of our own group or culture (the "in-group"), and against others (the "out-group") external to our own. Therefore, we typically discriminate in our own group's favor.

Most importantly, we tend to identify everything about the in-group as being normal (i.e., the way things ought to be done). Consequently, whenever we encounter people doing things a different way, we tend to see their actions not just as different but as deviant, even as wrong. We are particularly likely to do this when operating on our own turf, yet even when we are overseas we tend to take our own common experiences at home as the norm for how others ought to behave.

For example, although the United States and Mexico are geographically close to each other, the GLOBE clusters suggest that a significant cultural distance separates them. The GLOBE value scores for the two countries and the average for the entire worldwide sample (on a scale of 1 to 7) are as follows in Table 2.1.[18]

The table shows that the United States has a very high level of assertiveness, performance orientation, and gender egalitarianism as compared to the world average and to Mexico. Mexico, on the other hand, has very high uncertainty avoidance compared to the world average and the United States. It is easy to see how it might be difficult for individuals

TABLE 2.1

GLOBE DIMENSION	UNITED STATES	MEXICO	WORLD AVERAGE
Assertiveness	4.36	3.67	3.82
Institutional Collectivism	4.20	4.77	4.73
In-Group Collectivism	5.79	5.78	5.66
Future Orientation	5.35	5.74	5.49
Gender Egalitarianism	5.03	4.57	4.51
Humane Orientation	5.51	5.10	5.42
Performance Orientation	6.14	6.00	5.94
Power Distance	2.88	2.75	2.75
Uncertainty Avoidance	3.99	5.18	4.62

from one country to know how to behave socially in another country or to understand the process of making decisions in still another when those countries are from different groups.

As in the case of Barry and Miguel presented previously in the chapter, consider how an American and a Mexican with no prior cross-cultural experience might perceive each other from the standpoint of their own cultures. Despite some very different scores in both countries, individuals from each are likely to judge the other as though his or her own country represents the norm. Each will take "the way we do things at home" as a starting point. The American may find irritating Mexicans' emphasis on social activity, the slowness of their consultative decision making, their comfort with status differences between men and women, and their discomfort with any sort of ambiguity or with taking decisive action on their own initiative. For their part, the Mexican might see Americans as being self-centered, aggressive, and single-mindedly focused on performance.

The first step to cultural flexibility is to *understand your own culture* and how it affects your interpretation of the behavior of others. This is an important part—though far from the only part—of the cultural makeup and stereotyping that you most likely bring to each new cross-cultural situation you face. We have already suggested that you locate your own culture in terms of the Schwartz map or the GLOBE clusters. Think about your culture again in terms of all of its special features and idiosyncrasies. Try to look at it through the eyes of people from contrasting cultures.

Summary

This chapter describes how knowledge of what culture is and how it varies and affects behavior is the first stage of developing cultural intelligence. Culture is not a random assortment of customs and behaviors. It is the values, attitudes, and assumptions about appropriate behavior that are shared by people in specific groups. It is systematic and organized and has developed over time as a result of societies learning to deal with their common problems. Cultures can be defined according to their values—the fundamental beliefs that people within the culture share about how things should be and how one should behave. Culture is shared; it is passed on from one generation to the next. While it has a profound influence on behavior, the most important aspects of culture are invisible. A key feature of culture is that it categorizes others and us into in-groups and out-groups. This categorization of people into "them and us" underlies much cross-cultural behavior. There are several important dimensions along which cultures can be defined, the most important being individualism and collectivism. By understanding our own culture we can then make initial comparisons with others to understand areas of possible agreement or disagreement. The knowledge gained in this way is a necessary first step to becoming culturally intelligent. In subsequent chapters we link this knowledge with the important elements of mindfulness and cross-cultural skills.

CHAPTER 3

Mindfulness and Cross-Cultural Skills

FINDING HER FEET

Safiyah was a twenty-year-old Muslim exchange student from Malaysia, on her first visit to Australia. On Safiyah's first day in Sydney she dressed carefully, wearing an especially pretty hijab, and walked from her lodgings down to the nearby shopping mall. Wanting a few personal items, she entered a convenience store and gathered them, then went to the counter to pay. The shop assistant was busy solving some problem with the electronic till, and there was a young man ahead of Safiyah in the line. As she waited patiently behind him, Safiyah became aware of something deeply disturbing about his appearance. Even from behind him she could see that he was unshaven, and his hair was long and unkempt. He was poorly dressed, in a rather grubby sleeveless shirt and khaki shorts. Worst of all, he had no shoes on—his feet were bare!

Safiyah was aghast. Then, to her astonishment, she saw that the man was holding in his hands a huge box of chocolates that he clearly intended to purchase. The shop assistant finished her work on the till and priced the box of chocolates. "Twenty-two ninety-five," she said. The man drew out a brand-new leather wallet from the hip pocket of his shorts and pulled out a gold Visa card. The transaction was quickly completed. As the man waited for his receipt, he looked around the store. He must have noticed Safiyah staring at him, because as he turned to go, he said, in a voice that was puzzled rather than aggressive, "Are you all right?" The shop assistant and other customers turned to look. Safiyah muttered, "Yes . . . sorry." She was deeply embarrassed.

What had gone wrong for Safiyah in the store? There is a general difference in the way Malaysians and young Australians dress to go out in public. Untidy appearance in shops would be much less common in Malaysia than in Australia, but the element that made the difference extreme in this case was the Australian man's bare feet. In Malaysia it is assumed that the only reason a person might have bare feet is because he or she can't afford to buy shoes. In Australia and a few other countries, wearing no shoes, especially in summer, is considered comfortable, even fashionable, by many young people. In Malaysia, the man's appearance might denote a down-and-out or beggar. No wonder Safiyah was astonished to see the young man buying expensive chocolate; but in fact he might well have been a privileged, wealthy student.

In this chapter we look at how our cultural norms help but also hinder us in our dealings with others who are culturally different, by providing a "cultural cruise control" to guide our actions. We show that it is often necessary to break out of our cultural cruise control by practicing *mindfulness,* a kind of thoughtful attention to cues provided by what we experience, and as a result to develop new cross-cultural *skills.* The combination of knowledge (see Chapter 2), mindfulness, and cross-cultural skills is the basis of cultural intelligence.

Cultural Cruise Control

A good way of thinking about this is through the use of the term "script."[1] In the theater, a script tells the actor what he or she is supposed to say and sometimes how it should be said. In cultural rituals such as initiation ceremonies the script is often precise. But other scripts allow for individual interpretation (see discussion of "tight" versus "loose" cultures in Chapter 2).

There are, for instance, scripts for Americans and scripts for Chinese. For example, the workplace script of an American may allow her to be playfully disrespectful to a superior, but it would never be so for a Chinese. In the case at the beginning of this chapter, the scripted dress code for Malaysians going shopping is very different from that for young Australians.

Norms and scripts help us by telling us what to do. They prescribe patterns of behavior we feel comfortable with because we observe other members of our in-group practicing them. The real problems occur when the norms and scripts of one culture clash with those of another. This is because, in order to interact, we must not only act out our own scripts but also make sense of others' actions based on *their* scripts. To do this we have to break out of our scripted behavior and switch off our cultural cruise control. As Safiyah found, this is especially difficult in our initial experiences in a new culture.

Cultural cruise control means running your life on the basis of your built-in cultural assumptions. We call it cruise control because people let it happen automatically, without thinking about it. But it can be damaging because of the way it causes them to ignore other cultural signals.

In the case that opened this chapter, Safiyah is operating on cultural cruise control with regard to Malaysian conventions about dress. New to a different culture, she initially finds it impossible to move outside her standard assumptions that prescribe behavior in her culture and that label others according to how they dress. In the coming days she may be able to exercise the principles we describe in this chapter, get out of cultural cruise control, gain better insight into the norms of her Australian hosts, and improve her interactions with them. She needs to step aside as best she can from her own biases, observe what is going on around her without judgment, and talk to others in her new culture. She needs to tell herself, "I'm not in Kuala Lumpur now." By listening and learning, she can greatly improve her relationships in her new country. And she can do so without having to shed her own shoes, or her hijab!

Mindlessness

To develop cultural intelligence, you need to be able to suspend cultural cruise control and develop an alternative state of being called mindfulness.[2] A good starting point to understanding mindfulness is to examine its alternative—mindlessness—in the everyday activity of driving a car.

Driving is a complex skill, but we humans have learned to simplify it by developing sequences of complex actions that we perform competently without paying conscious attention. When driving, we can almost unconsciously steer, avoid obstacles, operate direction indicators, and brake when appropriate. While we drive we can simultaneously listen to the news on the radio, reflect on the day's work, plan the evening meal, have a conversation with a passenger, and even, in familiar territory, forget about navigating the car. Have you ever had the experience of arriving at your home in your car after following a familiar route and noting with surprise, "I'm here! How did I get here? I guess I was thinking about something else!"?

Mindlessness is not necessarily negative—in driving it simply means we drive without having our minds fully engaged on the job. If we can do so safely, why not? Mindlessness has advantages. It enables us to do more than one thing at a time, to ignore much of what goes on around us and to "get on with our lives."

However, mindlessness also has dangers. Mindlessness encourages us to rely on routine and prevents us from being flexible in changing circumstances. For example, businesspeople who have been successful in the past sometimes mindlessly continue with the same plans and methods that brought them success and fail to notice that circumstances have changed. Aid workers from developed countries mindlessly try to enlighten their counterparts in transition economies on "correct" actions in a market economy, even though such actions may be inappropriate for the different situation. Tourists traveling abroad mindlessly search menus for their "back-home" favorite dishes. These are examples of expecting cruise control to work in changing conditions for which it was not designed.

Sources of Cultural Scripts

We learn much about our culture from imitating others. As children, we imitate the attitudes and behavior of our parents and other role models.[3] We become aware of ideas and actions that are considered normal in our own culture. We encounter deliberate practices of socialization—at home, in school, and elsewhere—where we learn new scripts, often derived from the culture or subculture.

For most of us, cultural cruise control makes our own culture the center of our mental universe and causes us to regard all others as abnormal. Scripts from other cultures are not considered, and, if others practice them, we ignore or misunderstand them. Even if what we learn is simply unease in the presence of those from other cultures, this discomfort is likely to be built into our cruise control.

When we are with people with whom we share underlying cultural assumptions—most likely people from the same background and social class as well as culture—cultural cruise control tends to work well. As long as others share the same cultural grounding, we can take culture for granted and focus on other matters. But when we meet people whose cultural background is different, errors and misunderstandings quickly emerge, and our relationships are undermined.

Consider situations where someone has, to use an expression beloved by the English, "dropped a clanger" (that is, unwittingly said or done something offensive to the religion, ethnicity, background, or beliefs of someone else present). An example is putting out your hand to shake the hand of an orthodox Jew, not realizing that this familiarity is prohibited by his customs. Most clangers are caused by one person continuing to make the assumptions of his or her own culture without noticing that the other person has a different background and customs.

How Culture Affects Behavior[4]

Cultural programming also acts as a mental template against which new information is interpreted. We are not cameras: we do not take in neutral information from out there and reproduce it exactly on the film of our minds. We perceive information with cultural and other cues embedded in it and see it through the lens of our own preconceived frameworks. In the process, differences and distortions occur.

SELECTIVE PERCEPTION

At any given time, we can attend to only a fraction of the many ever-changing stimuli the world presents us. In cultural cruise control we rely on our mental programming and screen out all that is not directly relevant. Cultural conditioning teaches us what to perceive and what to ignore: people from different cultures can be presented with exactly the same situation and perceive it differently.

Suppose you are eating with someone at a restaurant, and your companion is talking about a business deal. If you are interested in business, you will pay close attention to the words. But if you are, for example, a fashion expert or a chef, you may be more interested in what your companion is wearing or eating, and if you are romantically interested you may attend to what they look like, and to cues that may tell you what they think of you. If you are from a collectivist society, you may be interested in the person's relationship with family or group, and if you are from an individualist society, in their personal attainments. Your culture is a key factor that focuses your attention.

SOCIAL CATEGORIZATION

Another key mental process for dealing with information is categorization. This process involves sorting other people (and ourselves) into different categories, just as postal workers sort mail into pigeonholes. Each hole might be labeled with a postal code. The postal worker does not read the name or address on the letter but glances only at the postal code in order to put the letter in the proper bin. In order to be similarly efficient, we categorize people based on limited information.

Often we categorize others on the basis of appearance. Speech—language, accent, vocabulary, content—is another important source of cues. We tend to make in-group and out-group categorizations (see Chapter 2); that is, we classify people according to whether they seem to belong, or not belong, to groups of which we ourselves are members.

Other key indicators of categories into which we might sort people are

- race and gender
- the extent to which a person stands out as different from others (for example, Europeans are obvious in rural Japan)
- being "typical" of a particular group
- a history of conflict with a group, leading to categorization as "not in our group"

Once we form a category, we perceive its members to be similar to each other, yet we continue to see differences among members of our own group. For example, an Asian may be aware of a broad category of "European," whereas a European will see many different categories within "European," for example, Anglo-Saxon, Celtic, Mediterranean, Scandinavian, and Slav, and also different national and regional categories.

STEREOTYPING

Putting people into categories influences our attitudes about and expectations of them.[5] We tend to perceive everyone in the group as having similar characteristics and behaviors. We may expect Americans to be noisy, Irish gregarious, and Japanese polite. These stereotypes need not be negative but often are, leading to prejudice and/or hostility. Perhaps the most obnoxious prejudice against others who are "not like me" is racism, partly because racial categorization is so easy.[6] Stereotypes of other nationalities may be intense, particularly when the group in question is prominent in one's experience. Much political conflict—for instance, Arab–Israeli, Indian–Pakistani, Shia–Sunni, Irish Catholic–Irish Protestant—creates and is supported by intense negative stereotypes of out-groups.

Stereotypes may be based on limited information or on the views of influential others. People who have never met anyone from another culture can hold intense stereotypes of that culture. Furthermore, stereotypes perpetuate themselves, because selective perception focuses attention on information that confirms our stereotypes and away from information that disconfirms them.

ATTRIBUTION

In attribution we move beyond simply observing and interpreting others to making inferences about *why* they behave as they do. Particularly important is the distinction between internal attributions, in which behavior is attributed to factors associated with the person (for example, "she punished her son because she is an aggressive person"), and external attributions, in which we believe behavior is caused by external circumstance ("she punished her son because he misbehaved").

When categorization and stereotypic expectations are combined with attribution, we get some interesting effects. For example, "she punished her son because she is Serbian, and Serbians are cruel and aggressive."

A common error is to attribute the behavior of members of an out-group to the same causes that would likely be true if members of our own in-group behaved the same way, as shown in the following case.

THE BOYFRIEND WHO WASN'T

Naoko, a female Japanese exchange student at a college in South Carolina, writes excitedly to her Osaka girlfriend: "Here in America, I have a new boyfriend! His name is Clive. He is good looking, with curly hair. I was taken to visit his parents' house, and he was very nice to me, looking after my every need. I think we will soon have a date."

Clive, meantime, confides to his friends: "Naoko seems to have gotten things all mixed up. I have a girlfriend already, and I don't want two. Sure, I was nice to her when she visited, but that was just normal politeness."

Clive comes from America's traditional Deep South, where social graces and effusive good manners have long been the norm. Clive was only acting as he had been brought up always to act in social situations. Unfortunately, the same type of behavior practiced in Naoko's culture would have been evidence of a romantic interest.[7]

In this case, cultural cruise control affected both parties. Clive continued to act automatically in the script of his own culture, noticing only too late the impression his behavior was making on his companion. Naoko continued to observe automatically through the lens of her own culture and made no allowances for the difference in background. Without either one meaning to, the two colluded to create a major misunderstanding. What was needed was for them to *switch off their cultural cruise control* and adopt a state of mindfulness in which they both become aware of the cultural significance of their own and the other's behavior.

Switching off Cultural Cruise Control

A pilot whose airplane is set on cruise control—automatic pilot—can rely on the expert programming built into the automatic system to keep the plane flying straight and level on the correct course, as long as conditions stay normal. But occasionally a change in conditions—a sudden weather hazard, a mechanical failure—will trigger warning signs. The pilot will snap out of mindlessness, switch off the automatic pilot, and devote full attention and skill to the problem.

A person from the United States who tries to drive a car in Japan or Britain, where the traffic travels on the left side of the road rather than the right and the driving controls are on the right side of the car not the left, will have to abandon some of the built-in rules and habits of driving in the United States. In novel cross-cultural situations, it is similarly imperative that we switch off our cultural cruise control. However, doing so is just the first step. Suspending cultural mindlessness directs your attention to cultural issues. It does not follow that you are attending to them in a productive way. To get maximum benefit requires a new set of active practices, which we call mindfulness.

Mindfulness

Mindfulness is such a common idea that many people do not appreciate how powerful it can be. It is actively *paying attention* to the present situation and its context. It means discarding our rigid mental programming. It does not mean abandoning who we are but rather using attention to become aware of differences and to think differently. It involves recognizing that despite cultural differences there will be many similarities between us and people from other groups, and that cultural differences do not matter all the time.

In cross-cultural interactions, mindfulness means simultaneously paying attention to the external situation, monitoring our own thoughts and feelings, and regulating the knowledge and skills we use.

MINDFUL ATTENTION

Mindful attention involves using all of the senses (for example, hearing the words that the other person speaks but also noting the expression on his or her face), viewing the situation with an open mind, and attending to the context to help interpretation.

MINDFUL MONITORING

Mindful monitoring means being aware of our own assumptions, ideas, and emotions, as well as noticing cues from the other people and tuning in to their assumptions, words, and behavior. It also means putting ourselves in other people's shoes as a means of understanding the situation and their feelings toward it, from the perspective of their cultural background rather than ours.

MINDFUL REGULATION

Mindful regulation means creating new mental maps of other people's personalities and cultural backgrounds to assist in responding appropriately to them, seeking out fresh information to confirm or disconfirm the mental maps, choosing not to respond automatically, and editing responses to be consistent with our goals.

Consider these examples:

Mindlessness—"After I finished the job, she started criticizing me. She is always criticizing me. She is Asian and doesn't understand how we do things here. So I stopped listening to her. She went on and on, and eventually I just walked out."

Mindfulness—"After I finished the job, she started criticizing the way I had done it. I listened to what she had to say; maybe she would have some good points to make. I paid attention to the tone of her voice and the way she looked: she didn't really seem angry, just concerned. I was aware that I hadn't done that sort of work before, that she was more experienced. I knew she would have to explain the problem to her boss, and I wondered how that would feel for her. She is Asian, and I knew she would not want to lose face. But she is so knowledgeable; I knew I could learn from her. I also knew she didn't like to be interrupted, so I waited patiently till she was finished. Then I apologized for my mistakes, thanked her for her feedback, and asked if she could monitor me while I did the job again."

Mindfulness is a mediating step that helps us to use knowledge to develop skillful practice. It gives us readiness to interact with people who are different. It gives us the background to communicate comfortably and accurately in ways that honor the backgrounds and identities of both parties. And it focuses our minds on the cross-cultural aspects of the situation.

Initially being mindful takes considerable effort. But over time being mindful can become a natural and normal way of being. We can't be mindful all the time, and we don't have to be. But mindfulness helps us to be in control and leads to greater freedom of thought and action.

Cross-Cultural Skills

Knowledge and mindfulness are key elements in cultural intelligence, but in themselves they are not enough. In practice, cultural intelligence is seen in and judged by *skilled behavior.* Cultural intelligence is not just a mind game—you have to be able to *perform.*

For example, in the case with which we started this chapter, it will be insufficient for Safiyah to learn Australian dress norms and pay more mindful attention to how things are normally done in her new country. She also needs to moderate her behavior such that any cultural discomfort she may feel is not on public display and so that she is able to interact suitably and develop good relationships. Australians, such as the shoeless young man she met, might likewise benefit from appreciating the expectations of those who are culturally different and taking those into account in deciding how to dress and how to act.

The third and last element of cultural intelligence is *cross-cultural skills.* The concept of skill can be applied to social behavior. In organizations, for example, the most common problems are not technical or administrative deficiencies but communication failures, misunderstandings in negotiations, personality conflicts, poor leadership style, and bad team-work—in other words, people interacting inadequately with each other.

Nowadays, many organizations regard social and interpersonal skills as key qualifications for employees. More than 70 percent of managers' time, in most cultures, is typically spent in interaction with superiors, subordinates, peers, clients, and others, in face-to-face conversations, meetings, telephone calls, and informal social settings.[8] Skilled interpersonal performance is vital, and many companies offer their employees skills training.

Most of us admire the social performance of colleagues and others who are outstanding in the art of interpersonal communication and relationship building. Each of us also has his or her own set of skilled social behaviors, which are closely related to the expectations and scripts of our own culture. Some of the social skills we develop in our own cultures may contain elements—such as willingness to initi-ate a conversation, interest in other people, and listening skills—that may assist us in other cultural settings. However, operating in other cultures also creates a new frontier for our social interactions, often requiring the development of new social performance.

Acquiring the skills of cultural intelligence does not mean becoming more skilled in a particular set of behaviors but rather building general skills that extend the range, or rep-ertoire, of skilled behaviors, and knowing when to use each one. Cultural difference extends the range of possibilities that we may face.[9] Skilled routines we have mastered effectively in one culture may be counterproductive in another, to the extent that we have to "unlearn" them in the new situation. Here is a case in point.

FRENCH DRESSING

Philippe LeBeau was a stereotypically dark, handsome Frenchman. He was known particularly for his charm toward women. This was particularly important in the Paris media company where Philippe worked as a manager, because the majority of employees were women.

Philippe had noticed that many of these women took pride in dressing fashionably. He would therefore compliment them fre-quently on their appearance—for example, "Marie, that is such a chic outfit! You look beautiful today." This kind of comment almost always gained him a smile, a blush, a thank you, and more importantly, he felt, increased cooperation from the woman he had complimented.

Philippe's company was taken over by a major international con-glomerate based in the United States, and to his delight Philippe was transferred for a two-year assignment in the company head-quarters in New Jersey. He was given a briefing on the United States and its different norms and was advised, for example, that touching other people, particularly those of the opposite sex, was much less acceptable there than in France. He therefore resolved to be careful about his habits of taking his female colleagues' hands in his, kissing them on the cheek, and the like.

In New Jersey, his new secretary, Anita Courtenay, was highly effective as well as strikingly beautiful. Like many of Philippe's French colleagues, she dressed extremely well. Philippe was careful to keep his physical distance from Anita as he had been taught, but he felt that her obvious glamour provided an opportunity to build a good working relationship. So in his customary French manner he would greet her every morning with a fresh compliment on her appearance. Her initial reaction was surprise. Then she would thank him politely and change the subject. But after a week or so she began to respond by frowning and pursing her lips. Philippe was puzzled. She really was an outstanding secretary as well as a beautiful woman. Did she think his compliments were insincere? And was it his imagination, or was she wearing outfits that were less chic with each passing day? Was she also using less makeup?

One morning he arrived at his office to find Anita seated at her desk, apparently wearing no makeup and with an outfit that was neat and tasteful but far from glamorous. Even in this modest attire, Anita looked fresh and lovely, and Philippe said so: "Anita, once more you are looking wonderful. My heart is beating faster, and I know that I will work better today because of it."

She looked at him with astonishment, then stood up. "Mr. LeBeau," she said levelly, "please stop making comments on my personal appearance. I am not here as a decoration, I am here as an employee. I take pride in what I do, but all you can talk about is the way I look. Can you imagine how that makes me feel? I have tried to discourage you, but you won't take a hint. And if you have any ideas about getting involved with me, you can forget them— I'm not interested. So from now on, can you please treat me with a bit more respect and professionalism?"

In this case, Philippe has developed a repertoire of skilled behavior that worked well in one cultural situation but, even when modified, broke down in another. His performance is based on a particular "French" view of the world, on ways of expressing himself probably developed from childhood, on sheer habit, and on having had the habit consistently rewarded. It will be hard for Philippe to erase the habits that don't work in his new environment and to replace them with new, more appropriate forms of social performance. First he will need to gain a better understanding of the norms of male-female interaction in his new culture (knowledge). Then he will have to pay more attention to the behavioral cues provided by Anita and the other women with whom he interacts (mindfulness). Last he will need to develop, experiment with, and refine new ways of behaving toward women.

The development of this new behavior involves developing a set of general skills. The general skills that research has shown are related to appropriate behavior in cross-cultural interactions are as follows:[10]

- relational skills
- tolerance for uncertainty
- empathy
- perceptual acuity
- adaptability

The specific behavioral skills that are required to operate across cultures span the gamut of interactions and interpersonal relationships in organizations.

Skilled Performance

To understand the skills aspect of cultural intelligence, think of yourself as a *performer*. The notion of skilled performance has been applied to many different areas of human endeavor. Diana Krall singing a jazz standard or Novak Djokovic hitting a perfect tennis serve epitomize the smooth and apparently effortless production of behaviors that exercise near-perfect control over parts of the physical world. These virtuoso performers have enormous physical and mental talent in their chosen fields, yet each has also spent many years of hard work perfecting her or his art. Djokovic's performance is built on numerous skills, such as manual dexterity and distance estimation, and Krall's on other skills, such as the ability to hear different musical tones and mastery of voice control. The performance of effective cross-cultural behavior is built on general skills, such as those indicated above, and sometimes on skills specific to particular cultural situations.

A key skill element in cultural intelligence is *adaptability.* Each situation will be unique and will involve interaction with unique people. As skilled social performers, we have to be able instantaneously to adapt our general approach and specific interactions to the particular characteristics of the situation and to the expectations of the other people involved. Effective cross-cultural behavior is not composed of fixed routines but of flexible abilities that can—with the guidance of mindfulness—be modified to meet new or changing conditions. Within every culture people vary in the extent to which they conform to underlying cultural norms. The culturally intelligent person's social performance draws on a repertoire of potential behaviors. By mindfully monitoring the environment, he or she is able to select, employ, and modify appropriate routines from this wide resource.

Summary

This chapter describes how our cultural programming affects our behavior and our interactions with others who are culturally different. Much of the time we base our actions on cultural cruise control, in which our mental programming directs our behavior without much conscious thought and allows us to continue to do things without actively thinking about them. However, in cross-cultural interactions this mindless behavior can cause problems. Through selective perception, stereotypic expectations, and inaccurate attributions, we may misjudge the behavior of others who are culturally different. To counteract the tendency to function on cultural cruise control, this book advocates practicing mindfulness, an active awareness that links knowledge about culture to appropriate behavior in cross-cultural situations. The culturally intelligent person also needs to increase his or her repertoire of skilled behaviors, particularly social behaviors, and to be able to deploy these appropriately in different cultural settings. The elements of knowledge, mindfulness, and skills enable the practice of cultural intelligence in skilled performance that is adapted to the particular cultural settings the individual faces.

CHAPTER 4

Making Decisions
across Cultures

Santoso, an Indonesian, and Alice, an Australian, are friends and business partners, working tough road-building projects in Indonesia, where Alice's civil engineering background and Santoso's local knowledge and financial skills have complemented each other. Now they find they have a major disagreement.

Two years ago, Adi Perkasa, a senior manager in the company who is independently wealthy, used his high status and connections in the area to secure for the company a major road-building project. Santoso and Alice saw the project as a godsend because they had been facing an uncertain period with few contracts. Moreover, due to the hard work and skill of certain staff, the project has been successful and has made a large profit. Believing in sharing good fortune with those who made it possible, Santoso and Alice have decided to set aside US$100,000 for distribution to the senior personnel involved. The questions they have to decide are who gets paid a bonus and how much?

Three staff members immediately stand out. Adi secured the contract but had little to do with its completion. Bambang, an engineer, wrote a brilliant plan for the project but thereafter was distracted by a looming family tragedy. He is from a poor background, has a large family, and struggles to pay his bills: recently his son suffered a brain tumor, and the family faces a bill for overseas treatment that is simply beyond their means. Finally, as the project manager, Rafi managed the project enthusiastically, leading and motivating his project team extremely well to far exceed the project objectives.

How should they distribute $100,000 to reward three such distinctive contributions? Alice suggests to Santoso that each of them should write down a suggested fair allocation and that they then use these starting points to negotiate what is fair. Santoso doesn't like that idea—he would prefer a general discussion of the three candidates first. But eventually he agrees. Alice thinks hard about the allocation and then writes down

> Adi: $10,000
>
> Bambang: $50,000
>
> Rafi: $40,000

When she looks at Santoso's sheet of paper, she is shocked. He has written

> Adi: $60,000
>
> Bambang: $10,000
>
> Rafi: $30,000

She looks at Santoso in disbelief. "You can't be serious," she says. "Adi is a lazy, aristocratic con man. And he is already rich—he doesn't need this money. Rafi made this profit for us. And what about Bambang—his plan was great, and what's more, he needs the bonus more than anyone else. How can you possibly justify giving all that money to Adi?"

Santoso shrugs his shoulders. "Adi is a very important person," he says. "He is well-connected. Our company is lucky to have him. Without him there would be no project, no profit, and no bonus for anyone. If he finds out we paid the others more than him, he will be insulted. He may leave. And then where will we find such contracts? As for Bambang, the family worries of others are no concern of ours."

Decision making is everyone's business. Each of us constantly makes decisions—which item on the menu to choose, which house to buy, whether or not to pursue a relationship. We choose from among alternatives all the time. Mostly, we think we are doing so by being logical. But it is often cultural patterns that determine both the way we make decisions and the decisions we make. In the case above, Alice structured the decision-making procedure rationally: she did her best to allocate fairly by applying normal Western principles of rewarding effort and performance but was probably influenced in deciding Bambang's reward by an ethic of humanitarianism. In contrast, Santoso wanted to discuss the problem before beginning to devise a solution, paid more attention to role and status than to performance, and dismissed the humanitarian aspect for someone not part of his in-group. Alice and Santoso are adhering to decision models that are characteristic of their cultural backgrounds.

Culture influences what is perceived as desirable and also how to achieve these goals. It determines how decision makers simplify the complex reality of decision making. In order to break out of their culturally based decision-making scripts, both Alice and Santoso need to learn from each other and develop their cultural intelligence.

The Rational Model

Decision making in many Western countries has been heavily influenced by the application of a linear type of formal logic called the *rational* model of decision making. We see this often in business. However, culture influences all decision making, be it at work, in the home, or elsewhere.

The rational model states that decision making operates— or should operate—in a sequence of steps. These involve

- *defining a problem:* for example, a leadership vacuum created by the resignation of the organization's chief executive officer (CEO)

- *generating a range of potential solutions:* for example, attracting a range of candidates for the vacant CEO job
- *applying systematic analysis to the potential solutions to predict which one will best satisfy predetermined criteria:* for example, subjecting CEO candidates to formal assessments to determine which would provide the best leadership
- *choosing and implementing the best alternative:* for example, selecting, appointing, and supporting the candidate for CEO who performs best on the assessments.[1]

This approach is the basis of management science and is implicit in the thinking behind such management decision-making techniques as linear programming, break-even analysis, feasibility studies, and strategic choice. Many individuals pride themselves on their powers of analysis and logic, and promote and defend their decisions accordingly. However, other decision-making models are possible. What would you think of a board chair who said that the new CEO had been selected for one of the following reasons?

"His father had the job before him—it's a company tradition."

"We liked her more than any of the other candidates."

"He comes from a good family and attended an excellent university."

"We asked all the employees, and she got the most votes."

"We prayed, and God showed us the correct choice."

"We hired him because he is the brother of a board member."

"We all know him well, and we know we can trust him."

"Through his wife, he has excellent political connections."

"We chose her because she offered the biggest payment."

"I don't really know why we appointed him. It just seemed like the right thing to do. It was intuitive."

A Western board acting thus might have its shareholders howling for blood. Yet all of the criteria above are common in one place or another, part of the fabric of business decision making. Even in the West they may be used more than we imagine but not acknowledged. Instead, those who make an appointment based on tradition, personal attractiveness, family background, popularity, nepotism, friendship, politics, graft, or intuition typically deny that these factors were considered, and cite "rational" grounds for the decision.

This adherence to a linear analytical model of decision making is part of a script or cultural cruise control (see Chapter 3) typically practiced by Westerners. In the bonus decision case study, this type of linear rationality is part of Alice's underlying philosophy. However, her Indonesian counterpart, Santoso operates from different assumptions, with a script that is more holistic and emphasizes the specific context of the situation.[2] Cultures often have different criteria against which to assess decision outcomes.

Can Westerners be sure that the analytical thinking in which they are indoctrinated by their society, their education, and their employing organizations is always the best basis for decision making? We think not. The West may have something to teach others about decision making, but it can also learn something from others in this diverse world.

In this chapter we focus first on the rational model, indicate some limitations in its use, and then show some alternatives that are used effectively in other cultures. We advocate a more flexible, culturally intelligent approach to decision making based on appreciating and using a diversity of methods.

Problems with the Rational Model

Quite apart from the alternatives used in non-Western cultures, the rational model of decision making is known to be imperfect.[3] It might work well if

- decision makers had clear unambiguous criteria to work toward (for example, short-term versus long-term profit, market share, employee safety, family harmony, self-fulfillment). In fact, criteria are seldom clear and are often in conflict.

- decision makers were agreed on rational models to understand the human elements involved in decisions. It is often easy to understand a mechanical or financial system in rational terms, but in systems involving people, agreement is difficult to reach.

- decision makers were capable of accurately defining the problem, generating a range of alternative solutions, accurately predicting the outcomes of all possible solutions, and manipulating huge amounts of relevant data. In fact, decision makers typically have limited capacity in all these areas. Much intended rational decision making gets replaced in practice by a "messier" process of "muddling through."[4]

- decision makers were unbiased enough to stick with the solution suggested by a rational analysis, even if they personally didn't like it.

- there was time to consider fully every possible alternative. Imagine, for example, trying to select a new home by evaluating every single house for sale in the city.

Even decision makers who pride themselves on their rationality can seldom overcome these difficulties. In practice, they adopt various decision-making strategies that are less than rational:

- They work *incrementally*, moving gradually toward a decision in small steps rather than performing a single powerful analysis.

- They create *heuristics*, simple rules of thumb that may or may not have a rational basis but that simplify the decision-making task.[5]

- They *satisfice*; that is, they choose a plausible alternative that they become aware of early, rather than continuing to look for the best alternative.[6]
- They procrastinate, they panic, and sometimes they avoid the decision altogether.

These forms of simplification are generally consistent across cultures. But there are also differences. For example, a common mental simplification or heuristic, called *availability*, is to rely on the ease of recalling something from memory and to give more weight to easily imagined events in making a judgment. But because this heuristic is based on experience, it can vary across cultures. For example, Thais would probably give a higher estimate than would Americans of the worldwide rate of death by being trampled by a water buffalo.

In some cultural settings decisions may be appropriate that are based on tradition or consensus or family advantage or custom. And even if we could get around all the impediments to rationality mentioned above, the meaning of rationality differs across cultures, and a decision made without reference to cultural factors is at least as likely to fail as a decision made purely on cultural grounds.

Rational decisions often fail to be made and implemented because they are unacceptable. It has been wisely stated that the measure of a decision's adequacy is a function of its quality and its acceptability.[7] Trying to approximate rationality may result in a high-quality decision, but that decision also has to be *implemented,* usually by people other than the decision maker. Any couple who has tried to buy a house knows that a logical case is useless against a partner's statement such as "I just don't like the feel of it," and that the house must be acceptable to both partners. If those involved do not accept the decision, they will not be committed to making it work, and, however "rational" it is, it will probably fail. In the bonus decision case, Alice and Santoso need to work together toward a solution that, despite their different cultures, they both find acceptable.

Culture thus imposes limits on what decisions can realistically be implemented. In some countries the appointment of a woman to a high-status position—however suitable she may otherwise be—is unacceptable, so any woman appointed will most likely fail because of the unwillingness of others to work with her. In other countries the implementation of work practices that involve breaking religious taboos cannot be tolerated, no matter how rational they may be.

An important limitation on rational decision making comes from the cultural dimension, identified in Chapter 2, called *collectivism*. Collectivism calls into question who makes the decision, how it is made, and who benefits from it. In both individualist and collectivist cultures, it is acceptable for decisions to be made by individuals. However, in a collectivist culture the society must also have a norm of hierarchy, and the decision maker should be of high status (as in China). But in collectivist cultures with more egalitarian norms (such as Israel) it is expected that the collective will be properly informed, consulted, and involved.

It is important for Western decision makers to suspend, in part, their own notion of rationality as the basis for decision making, to be mindful of the specifics affecting decision making in other cultures, and to learn to reinterpret rationality to accommodate local habits and constraints.

Motivation and Goals

Decisions are also affected by the motives and goals of those who make them.[8] For example, a manager deciding who to appoint as her assistant might mainly seek to improve the organization's performance, or to remain popular with staff, or to maintain power by appointing a weak subordinate, or to follow tradition. Such motives vary with culture.

In Western cultures, many would-be rational decision makers often pride themselves on their ability to set aside their personal motivations and to rely instead on applying logic to achieve a good result. For example, they might choose the candidate they think has the best qualifications for a job rather than the one they like the most or who is a family member. But the non-Western rational model might instead consider factors such as a personal relationship of the candidate to the decision maker and the social context of the decision. After all, who can I trust more to do a good job than a member of my own family?

A fundamental difference such as individualism/collectivism can dramatically affect decisions. People from individualist cultures generally assert their own rights and ideas and resist group pressure, whereas those from collectivist cultures are more influenced by the context and the ideas of others. For example, in one research study,[9] people from collectivist Brazil were more likely than those from the individualist United States to forego a personal financial benefit in order to visit a sick friend. Another important product of individualism is high individual self-esteem and optimism. For example, Americans are much more likely to overestimate their abilities, chances of success, and so on than are the collectivist Japanese. But Japanese are more likely to believe that their judgments are shared by others.[10]

Culture also determines which decisions will be acceptable. Individual incentives for productivity may get good results in an individualist culture but not in a collectivist one. But to those in an individualist culture, participative group discussions that slow down decision making may be irksome. In a high power-distance culture, people expect and may even welcome autocratic behavior from bosses, but in a low power-distance culture, they will reject such behavior. Decision makers need to read the motivation, particularly the culture-based motivation, of staff.

In addition, by considering culturally based motivational

differences, we may be better able to understand the decision-making methods and criteria used by our counterparts from different cultural backgrounds. In the bonus decision case, Santoso and Alice are influenced by the collectivism and individualism of their respective cultures. Each acts according to the motivation of his or her cultural group. Both fail to exhibit cultural intelligence.

Selection and Allocation Decisions

IT'S WHO YOU KNOW THAT COUNTS

Jan Moore, European area manager for Clarkson Equipment Corporation (CEC), telephones Craig Finley, CEC's manager for Russia: "Hi Craig. Sorry, but I've been looking at your latest report, and there's a problem with the Slovaski project."

"Oh? Sorry to hear that. What problem?"

"This funding request, made by Sasha, the project manager, to send his new management trainee to London to get an MBA, all paid for by us."

"What of it? We've done that for promising juniors before."

"Turns out he's Sasha's son!"

"Oh, that."

"And that's not all. I've been going through all the last few years' appointments to the Slovaski project. They're nearly all friends and relations of Sasha's. And the promotions—his relations are going up the organization chart like shooting stars! It's sheer nepotism, Craig."

"That's the way they do things round here, I'm afraid. Sasha's very good at what he does. And he makes sure his protégés do a good job."

"Look, Craig, this can't go on. The company has a standard hiring procedure, and Sasha's breaking every rule in the book. Weren't you supposed to introduce our standard hiring practices— you know, job requisitions, advertisement of vacancies, candidate résumés, line managers conducting interviews, and so on?"

"I did, but the Russians don't like them. They ignore them."

"Oh, for heaven's sake! Craig, you were instructed three years ago to appoint an experienced HR manager over there to implement and control the hiring policies. Why haven't you done it?"

"Because I know it would be a disaster. There would be huge resentment, and not just from Sasha. Look, Jan, we're operating in an Asian culture here. Western standards don't always work. If hiring people you have known for a long time and therefore trust is a local custom, you can't change it overnight. And you probably don't need to change it."[11]

Staff selection decisions are among the most common in organizations. In the example, the Westerner, as usual, proposes an analytical model focused on candidates' behavior. The Russians prefer to rely on more holistic and subtler contextual cues of suitability.

Here, we can contrast the Western view that what counts is *what you can do* with the Eastern belief that what counts is *who you are*. In our initial case, Santoso's awarding of the highest bonus to the person with the highest status rather than to the biggest contributor is similar. In China, the network of a candidate's relationships, his or her *guanxi*,[12] can be critical to selection for a job and ability to perform in it. *Guanxi*, though, is more complex and subtle than a simple relationship. It is likely to exist as part of a network of family and personal connections and to involve delicate patterns of mutual obligation.

In the West, such things are thought of as favoritism or nepotism and are frowned upon; rather than relying on their connections, candidates are expected to demonstrate their personal suitability. The East/West difference may be increased by the current Western fashion—often built into local legislation—for equal employment opportunity, meaning opportunity based solely on the Western criterion of individually assessed qualifications for the job. However, even this Western ideal can be affected by subconscious biases favoring one group over another.

Other cultural differences in selection practice are subtler. In one recent European research study,[13] the ability to do the job was the main criterion across a number of countries, but "ability" was differently defined, with egalitarian Scandinavian countries putting a lot of emphasis on interpersonal skills, whereas countries emphasizing status differences paid more attention to age.

Reward allocation decisions, such as that in the initial case, require making decisions that balance equality against equity. Suppose several people collaborate on a project, but some use more skill, work longer hours, and make more effort than others. An equitable allocation will distribute rewards in relation to responsibility, time, effort, and so on. An equal allocation will reward all participants equally just for contributing. Individualist cultures generally favor equitable solutions, whereas collectivist cultures tend to favor equal ones. Collectivists are also more likely to take into account need as a criterion.

Ethics and Decision Making

THE TRADE PERMIT

Mohammed is an official in a Middle Eastern country. His job is to review applications for trading permits issued to overseas visitors. He has to ensure that all the appropriate criteria are met. If they are, he will normally grant the permit.

Mohammed's salary is extremely low. Relying on his salary alone, Mohammed would be unable to provide for his family. Fortunately there is relief for him in the system: he is good at his job, and it is customary for applicants to show their appreciation for his service by giving him small sums of money. Many applicants are Americans and Europeans from wealthy multinational companies, which can easily afford these additional costs. The arrangement is understood by all those involved, including Mohammed's superiors, and works to the advantage of all.

Recently, however, Mohammed has had some difficulty working with John O'Connell, who has recently arrived as the representative for an Irish company seeking to build an export-import business. When O'Connell presented his application, it was impeccable. However, he showed no signs of offering a financial accommodation. Perhaps, Mohammed thought, this was just an oversight. He told O'Connell that some further paperwork was needed and that he should come back in a few days.

O'Connell has been back twice. Each time he has become more irritated at the delays, but despite hints from Mohammed, he still has not offered any cash. So Mohammed continues to prevaricate: if Mr. O'Connell will not play the game according to the established rules, he will have to accept the consequences.

Back at his office, John O'Connell calls an old friend, a man with experience in the country in question. The friend immediately realizes what the problem is and advises John how much he should offer and how he should make the offer. John becomes angry.

"But that's bribery!" he exclaims. "Pure corruption."

"No, it's just the way these people do things," says the friend. "Think of it as a tip."

In the global business environment, as in life generally, almost every decision has an ethical component. The press regularly tell us of ongoing ethical crises in many countries: politicians and business executives pillaging their countries and companies or maximizing "perks," lies and deception practiced against shareholders, "pork-barrel"[14] politics; bribery and corruption in governmental institutions, embezzlement; credit card and computer fraud; tax avoidance on a gigantic scale by both companies and individuals. But different societies often have very different views of what behavior is morally unacceptable. Monetary payoffs to officials in return for favors granted—the essence of the above case— represent just such an issue. The following are examples of common decisions that present global organizations with ethical dilemmas:

- Moving production to a foreign country to take advantage of cheap labor, resulting in exploitation and dangerous working conditions.

- Discouraging union organizing in countries where unions are not well established.

- Abiding only by the minimum environmental protection laws imposed by the country in which the company is operating, standards that may be much lower than those in the company's own culture.

- Promoting dangerous products (such as cigarettes) in foreign markets when demand declines at home.

- Doing business in a country with a repressive government.

- Imposing a global ethical norm developed by the headquarters of the firm.

- Advertising luxury goods in less developed countries.

However, you don't have to be at the top of the organization, or even in an organization, to face ethical dilemmas. Whether to pay unofficial inducements, what level of expenses to claim, whether to accept gifts from prospective suppliers, how much to claim on your theft insurance when your house is burgled—all these issues raise ethical questions. Those doing business internationally or dealing with staff or colleagues from different cultures quickly realize that what they think is morally correct erodes in the face of differing cultural values and norms for behavior. They often have difficulty in reconciling their own ethical standards with local practices, or, when invited to do something they truly believe to be wrong, in saying no.

Many decisions that cross countries or cultures are ethically ambiguous. Consider the common decision of organizations in economically advanced countries to relocate manufacturing in developing countries in order to achieve lower labor costs. Here is how such a decision might be perceived by (a) a manager from a developed country making such a decision in order to keep his company in business and (b) an activist concerned about the welfare of the people in the developing world.

> Businessman: "If we do not make this decision, we will go out of business, totally failing the shareholders who have put their trust in us. Everyone will lose their jobs, not just those in our European factory. We would be bringing to the people of the region of Vietnam where we seek to set up our factory an opportunity to participate in the Western dream of secure employment. We will pay a competitive wage. No one will be forced to work for us—they will do it because they know they are better off that way. We are helping them! But we cannot pay more. That would enable our competitors to take our market away, and everyone would suffer, including our Vietnamese employees. Our extension to Vietnam, you see, is totally ethical."

> Activist: "Your company is a fundamentally immoral organization, interested only in generating huge profits for its managers and shareholders. It seeks to move into Vietnam only because it knows it can exploit the people there. It will pay them wages that they can scarcely live on, force them to work long hours, and neglect their health and safety needs. If the company really wants to help the Vietnamese people, why doesn't it double the proposed wages and ensure reasonable working conditions? It could do that and still make a huge profit. But multinationals don't think this way because they are fundamentally unethical."

Who is right? Both! The two protagonists are proceeding from very different frames of reference. Interestingly, though, each party is seeking to do right by the Vietnamese workers involved.

To the activist, the concept of profit is immoral. Her radical analysis of "big business" focuses particularly on multinational companies because they use inter-country differences in areas such as labor costs, pollution control, and ability to get their way with government authorities as a basis for making big decisions—such as relocation—in the logical pursuit of profitability. This is part of a wider belief by businesspeople that in the end striving for profit is good for everyone—including the Vietnamese workers—because it causes economic systems to become more efficient and makes goods cheaper. While different cultures tend to have different views of business freedom and control, the moral questions separating this businessman from the activist cut across cultural boundaries, and the attitudes and institutions that support them are international.

The situation described above represents perhaps the most difficult ethical dilemma that global managers face. The question is "Should I follow a practice that is allowed in a foreign country but not in my own?" Managers commonly try to answer this question in three ways.[15]

- The first tries to evaluate the consequences of the decision and calculate the maximum benefit for the most people. This is what the businessman was arguing in defense of moving his factory to Vietnam. Many Vietnamese people would benefit, as well as the businessman's own shareholders. However, as indicated by the response of the activist, benefit is often in the eye of the beholder.

- The second approach is to rely on some moral rule. We all learn such rules as part of our cultural socialization, and these rules are often apparent in religious teachings. An example is the idea of treating others as you would like to be treated. However, the obvious problem with moral rules is finding a set of rules upon which all cultures can agree. For example, even in cultures as similar as the United States and Canada, strong differences in opinion exist with regard to the right of the state to put someone to death.

- The final method of answering ethical questions is the culturally relative approach. This approach suggests that ethical behavior varies from one culture to the next. While seemingly consistent with our general recommendations for being culturally intelligent, this approach is insufficient to deal with the ethical dilemmas of global managers making decisions across cultural boundaries. While many differences in business practice are in fact related to the cultural norms of a society, cultural relativity can make it possible for people to justify reprehensible behavior based on culture.

CULTURALLY INTELLIGENT DECISIONS

What then is the individual who wants to make an ethical decision to do? Not surprisingly, we suggest that the steps to cultural intelligence will also lead to more ethical decision making across cultures.

The first step is *knowledge*. We need to understand our own mental programming concerning what is ethical. What do we believe is proper behavior and why do we believe it? We also need to be aware that people in other cultures hold the values that are prevalent in their society.

The second step is being *mindful* of the ethical component of decisions. Who is likely to benefit, and who will be harmed by the decision? Mindfulness also means paying attention to all the factors that might influence the decision. These include the relative level of economic development in a society. The mindful decision maker will ask, "Would this practice be acceptable in my country at a similar level of economic development? Is this practice a violation of some fundamental human right?"[16]

The cross-cultural *skills* of the culturally intelligent decision maker will include a repertoire of behaviors that recognize value differences across cultures but are consistent with self-chosen ethical principles. These principles will develop over time as the individual gains knowledge and practices mindfulness. He or she will uphold these non-relative values and rights regardless of majority opinion and will act in accord with these principles. Doing so will often require creative solutions to ethical dilemmas. For example, one organization, while yielding to the cultural norm of employing children under the age of fifteen in its factories in a developing country, also provided time off and monetary support to allow these children to acquire a basic education.

Summary

This chapter describes decision making in cross-cultural context. Perhaps the world is gradually accepting a Western-style linear analytical approach to decision making, but this approach is not universal. Globalization is driven by a relentless logic of business profitability, and the process of globalization has been dominated by organizations based in the United States and Western Europe attempting to impose that logic in Latin America, Asia, Eastern Europe, and the Middle East. However, because people in different cultures have different mental programming, the ways in which they simplify the complex process of decision making are likely to be different. Decisions are also affected by the motives and goals of the decision maker, which are based on culturally different values. The culturally intelligent person is better able to understand the decision-making methods and criteria used in other cultures. Almost all decisions have an ethical component because some stakeholders benefit and others do not. The culturally intelligent decision maker is able to balance the culturally relative nature of ethics while upholding fundamental human rights.

CHAPTER 5

Communicating and Negotiating across Cultures

Consider these four vignettes of cross-cultural living, all of them authentic experiences.[1]

- Brits Clay and Joanne arrive in Auckland, New Zealand, for their holiday—the first time they have ever visited. They are monolingual and like the fact that New Zealand is an English-speaking country. They take an airport bus to the city center. They know their hotel is close by, so as they leave the bus they ask the driver for directions. "That's easy," says the driver. "Just follow the footpath a hundred meters and you're there." He closes the bus door and drives off. Clay and Joanne look around. There is no footpath in sight. What on earth did the driver mean?

- Stephanie, an American student, shares a dormitory room with Anong from Thailand. They get on well. Then, after they have lived together for several weeks, Anong abruptly announces that she has applied for a transfer to another room. Stephanie is surprised and upset and asks Anong why she wants to move. Anong is reluctant to speak but eventually says that she can't stand Stephanie's noisiness, loud stereo, late visitors, and untidiness. Stephanie is even more surprised; all this is new to her. "Couldn't you have told me this sooner?" she asks. "Maybe I could have done something about it."

- Ben is serving customers at a Texas drive-in fast-food outlet. It is hot, there are many customers, and Ben is tired. A black man drives up. He has ordered a cheeseburger combo. He pays Ben and takes his change. As Ben reaches for the order, the man inquires whether Ben is having a good day. "Not particularly," Ben replies honestly. The man looks concerned, says sympathetically, "Me, either," and inquires after Ben's health. Ben eyes the line of cars behind and says, "Sorry, sir, could you move on? We have a lot of customers to serve today." He hands over the order, but the man looks at the food incredulously, almost disgustedly. He glares at Ben and drives off. Ben stares after him in surprise. "What did I do wrong?" he wonders.

- Harry, an American economist, is on a study tour in China. He visits an economic planning institute where a Chinese economist, who is interested in American forecasting techniques, invites him to return to China to give seminars. Harry is very interested in the offer, and says so, but adds that he has to check with his institute to get approval. Back in the United States, he is granted the necessary clearance and sends a message to China indicating that he is definitely available. But the Chinese never contact him again.

These cases, to which we will return, demonstrate communication failures that led to the breakdown of relationships, and all have cultural origins.

Communication is the fundamental building block of social experience. Whether selling, buying, negotiating, leading, or working with others, we communicate. And although the idea of communicating a message seems simple and straightforward—"You just tell it straight. And you listen."—when it comes to figuring out what goes wrong in life, communication failure is by far the most common explanation.

Communication uses *codes*, systems of signs in which each

sign signifies a particular idea, and *conventions,* agreed-upon norms about how, when, and in what context codes will be used. If people do not share the same codes and conventions, they will have difficulty communicating with each other. And codes and conventions are determined mainly by cultures. The most obvious example of unshared codes is different languages.

The communication breakdowns in our opening vignettes can be explained by cultural differences:

- In the first case Clay and Joanne are unaware that a "footpath" in New Zealand is what in the UK would be called "pavement" or what Americans call a "sidewalk." This is an example of different *codes.*

- In the second case of the student whose Thai roommate moved out, culture and custom interfered with communication. In their upbringing, Americans are encouraged to be active, assertive, and open, and to expect the same in others. In *their* upbringing, Thais are encouraged to be passive and sensitive, and they too expect the same in others. The Thai expected the American to be sensitive to her feelings; the American expected the Thai to say what her feelings were. When neither behaved as expected, the relationship broke down. This is an example of different *conventions.*

- In the third case the black man was newly arrived from Ghana. Being from a collective culture, he was naturally being sociable with Ben. But Ben passed the food to him with his left hand, which is considered rude in Ghana. This is an example of different *codes* AND *conventions.*

- Harry, whose invitation to return to China was never followed up, failed to appreciate the meaning of his own communication in Chinese culture. A Chinese person saying that he had to check with his office might be communicating that either he is a low-status person who has to check everything with bureaucrats or that he is not really interested in visiting. Here, the Chinese economist may have assumed the same about Harry. Chinese people seldom say no even when that is what they mean. Instead, they have numerous polite ways of indicating it. This is another example of different *codes* AND *conventions*.

In all of the vignettes, *both* parties failed to appreciate the codes and conventions of the other. If either one had been more culturally intelligent and had acted accordingly, the bad feelings and/or negative outcomes might have been avoided.

How Cross-Cultural Communication Works

In communication, the communicator transmits meaning through messages to others ("receivers") who interpret them. The process is shown in Figure 5.1.

When the receiver in turn becomes the communicator, the process is reversed. The channel may be spoken or written words, or nonverbal behavior such as gestures or facial expressions. Face-to-face conversations, meetings, telephone calls, documents, and e-mails may all be used. Successful communication occurs when the meaning encoded in the message is accurately perceived and understood. Skills of communicating and listening, selection of an appropriate channel, and the absence of external interference are all important.

Cultural differences threaten communication by reducing the available codes and conventions shared by sender and receiver. Figure 5.1 represents culturally based elements in the sender's and receiver's backgrounds, such as their language, education, and values.[2] The cultural field creates the relevant codes and conventions.

Language

Language is the most obvious code for communicating. In language, combinations of sounds represent elements of

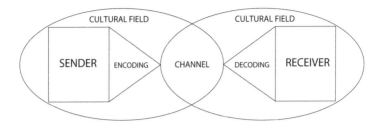

FIGURE 5.1. Cross-cultural communication process
Source: Based on Schramm (1980)

meaning and can be combined to form complex messages. Most languages contain speech conventions, subtleties, and figures of speech apparent only to experienced speakers.

The essence of language is that sender and receiver should share the code. But the development and mobility of humankind has created thousands of different languages, plus different dialects and adaptations of many of them.[3] Most people have only one language, which they have used since early childhood, and even accomplished linguists are usually fluent in only a few. Moreover, psychologists have determined that the best time to acquire new languages is before age ten, after which we become progressively less able to adapt.[4]

In addition, the everyday use of any language normally goes beyond any simple single code. Languages are living entities that change to accommodate the different groups who use them, and they also change depending on the social circumstances in which they are used. For example, among young speakers of English, language has become more direct and dramatic, so that

"She accused me of breaking the window. I said I hadn't."

is now

"She's like, 'You trashed the window!' I'm like, 'No way it was me!'"

Within cultures, different groups have their own vocabularies, slang, accents, and dialects. Technical groups may develop and use their own jargon to communicate with each other while distancing themselves from outsiders. Another common convention is euphemism, where potentially impolite connotations are replaced with less explicit words. An example is the English convention of saying that someone has "passed away" rather than died.

Finally, in everyday conversation most people mindlessly use proverbs, maxims, and even slogans or catchphrases heard on television. For example, "it's a no-brainer," "it ain't over 'til the fat lady sings," and "it's not rocket science." Such expressions may genuinely puzzle outsiders.

Finding Common Language Codes

People seeking to communicate with each other without any overlapping language codes face a major barrier. They can employ interpreters, but this is time-consuming and expensive, and complicates the communication process.

Learning and using a foreign language has benefits beyond simply overcoming the language barrier. Most people appreciate the efforts that others may have made to learn their language. So even though your fluency in another language may be limited, the fact that you have made the effort may generate goodwill.[5] In addition, language often conveys many subtleties about a culture that a person with high cultural intelligence might notice and use.

However, becoming fluent in another language takes substantial study and practice, particularly if that language is very different from your own. Language learners often find that when using the new language they feel stressed and distracted, and that their lack of fluency may unfairly undermine their credibility. In contrast, fluency may lead to the speaker being perceived, sometimes mistakenly, as being competent in other areas, such as overall cultural intelligence.[6]

A Common Organizational Language

One byproduct of historical Anglo-American economic dominance and the unwillingness of British and American people to learn new languages has been to make English the accepted international language of business, and the learning of English a major global village activity. This change facilitates international business communication, but, as discussed ahead, has some less positive effects when it is adopted as a common organizational language.

In a move to create a mutually accessible language to unite a workforce that speaks different languages many firms have adopted English as a common language for the organization as noted in the following story.

ENGLISH ONLY AT RAKUTEN

In 2010, Hiroshi Mikitani, CEO of Japan's largest online retailer (Rakuten), mandated that English would be the official company language, affecting 7,100 Japanese employees. He believed that this new policy would help Rakuten to become the world's number one Internet services company. Rakuten had grown through mergers and acquisitions in France, Germany, and the United States, as well as joint ventures throughout Asia. Mikitani demonstrated his seriousness about the change by announcing it to employees in English. By the next day, cafeteria signs, elevator directories, and so on were replaced, and employees were told they must demonstrate competence in English within two years or risk demotion or dismissal. By 2012, half of Rakuten's Japanese employees could communicate adequately in English, and 25 percent were doing business in English on a regular basis. In 2015, the average score for Rakuten employees on the Test of English for International Communication (TOEIC) indicated advanced fluency. Thus Rakuten has accomplished something that the Japanese education system has been trying to do for years—get Japanese people to speak English competently.[7]

Not every firm is as radical in their approach as Rakuten, but language standardization is being driven by the globalization of tasks and resources, by cross-border mergers and acquisitions, and by competitive pressures.[8] Advocates of a common language (English) say that it improves coordination and integration, shapes the organizational image and gives organization members a sense of belonging. On the other hand, non-English speakers may feel a loss of status in the organization, resulting in resentment and distrust of native English speakers, more comfort with non-native speakers, anxiety about performing well, and concerns about job advancement. As a result, regardless of organizational attempts at becoming monolingual, the "common language" goal is often not widely shared.

Learning English as an additional language (EAL) is challenging. The language's richness of vocabulary and numerous synonyms can cause EAL speakers great difficulty. The simple word "fly," for example, can mean an annoying insect, a means of travel, or an important part of men's trousers.[9] Those who speak only English owe a debt to the millions of people around the world who have gone out of their way to learn to understand, read, speak, and write in English.

A person fluent in English who is communicating with a less skilled English speaker should communicate in standard terms and avoid jargon, obscure language, and assumptions about the other person's comprehension. Culturally intelligent people adapt their language to be in harmony with the other person's vocabulary and style.

Some EAL speakers, particularly those from cultures that typically avoid losing face, pretend to understand when they really do not. In these situations parties need to be especially aware of barriers and limitations in their sending and receiving, and to check whether messages have gotten through.

The following are some brief guidelines for improving communication with EAL speakers.

- Enunciate carefully.
- Avoid colloquial expressions.
- Repeat important points using different words.
- Use active verbs and avoid long compound sentences.
- Use visual restatements such as pictures, graphs, and tables.
- Hand out written summaries of your oral presentation.
- Pause frequently, and do not jump in to fill silences.
- Take frequent breaks, and allow more time.
- Do not attribute poor grammar or mispronunciation to lack of intelligence.
- Check for understanding by encouraging speakers to repeat concepts back to you.
- Don't embarrass speakers, but encourage and reinforce their participation.[10]

EXPLICIT AND IMPLICIT COMMUNICATION

There is a Western view that individuals perceive something called the truth and should state it. Convention also prescribes that communication should use explicit, direct, unambiguous verbal massages. But in other cultures—for example, many Middle Eastern and Asian cultures—there is no absolute truth, and politeness and desire to avoid embarrassment often take precedence. This makes communication implicit and indirect. In the direct convention, most of the emphasis is on the *content* of the communication—the words. In the indirect convention, the *context* is more important—for example, the physical setting, the previous relationships between the participants, and nonverbal behavior.

The direct convention tends to be the norm in countries with individualist cultures, the indirect in countries with collectivist cultures. Understanding indirect communication in collectivist cultures may sometimes involve learning another code. The following examples show ways of saying no politely and indirectly. In some cases a low-CQ individual would think that the answer might be "yes."

SAYING "NO" IN RESPONSE TO
"HAS MY PROPOSAL BEEN ACCEPTED?"[11]

Conditional "yes"	If everything proceeds as planned, the proposal will be approved.
Counter-question	Have you submitted a copy of your proposal to the ministry of . . . ?
Criticizing the question	Your question is very difficult to answer.
Refusing the question	We cannot answer this question at this time.
Tangential reply	Will you be staying longer than you had originally planned?
Yes, but	Yes, approval looks likely, but . . .
Delayed answer	You should know shortly.

The problems associated with explicitness of communication extend beyond face-to-face communication. The use of e-mail can increase these problems. E-mail requires turn-taking, that is, one sends a complete message and then awaits a reply. This works for low-context cultures, where the meaning is mostly expressed in the words; but e-mail strips away the context of the communication, making it more difficult to understand implicit meanings because one can't get clarification or read between the lines.

VERBOSITY AND SILENCE

Cultures vary in their conventions about *how much* and *how loudly* one should talk. Americans are notorious for talking a lot and loudly. But silence can be used deliberately and strategically. Japanese negotiators use silence as a means of controlling negotiating processes, whereas Finns use it as a way of encouraging a speaker to continue. In some cultures silence can show respect. Interpreting silence accurately is important.

Nonverbal Communication

The café in Athens was picture-perfect: checkered tablecloths, white walls, Mediterranean atmosphere. It was morning, so there were no customers. Behind the counter was Dimitri's mother. I'd seen her in Dimitri's photos.

"Mrs. Theodoridis?"

She turned toward me, puzzled.

"I'm Ray. From Australia. Your son Dimitri . . ."

She smiled broadly. "Oh, Ray! Yes! You Ray! Oh yes, Dimitri write me that you come to Greece. Oh, come, come! Sit! I bring you some coffee."

She motioned me to a table. Suddenly she frowned. "Oh! Maybe you no like Greek coffee? Maybe you want ouzo?"

She was fussing over me. We Australians can't stand being fussed over. But I stayed polite.

"Coffee would be great, thank you."

She nodded and went into the kitchen. I sat at the table. She came back with the coffee and stood opposite me. She was speaking to me warmly.

"Dimitri tell me you *so* help him when he move to Australia, with his English and everything." She put the coffee on the table and sat down opposite me, leaning toward me. She seemed too close. I could smell her perfume. I leaned back a little. We Australians like to keep our distance.

"So." Suddenly she placed both her hands over one of mine. "How you like Athens?" Before I could answer, she moved her right hand, took a gentle hold of my cheek, and shook it affectionately. "You find girlfriend, yes?"

This was not what I had expected. I had envisaged a more formal conversation, at a respectable distance, about Dimitri. Instead she had her hands all over me. Her eyes seemed to be staring right through me. And she was asking about my love life! What business was it of hers?

"Well, Mrs. Theodoridis," I managed, "I . . . er . . . um . . ." She was leaning toward me, close, intense. "I've only been here a couple of months."

"Yes, Ray, that's right." She was speaking to me as to a child. Now she put both her hands on my face, and leaned even closer. "You find nice Greek girl, settle down." She released me and leaned back, considering. "Some nice Greek girls. You have good salary at Constantine Shipping, yes?" She sipped her coffee. I was thinking, what *is* it with this woman? She is altogether too familiar. Better be polite, though.

"Well, Mrs. Theodoridis, I . . . er . . . haven't really thought about settling down."

"Yes, Ray, that's right." Why was she agreeing with everything I said? "Better be careful. Some of these Greek girls, they want big diamond ring, or fancy church wedding." Again she leaned toward me, put her hand under my chin, and looked at me intensely. "Are you religious, Ray?"

Bugger me, I thought, I've just met her, and already she's asking about my personal life, my money, and my religion! I felt confused, embarrassed, and hot. What to do?

Then I had a brainwave. Play for time! "Ah, well, Mrs. Theodoridis. Maybe I will have that ouzo after all."

"Aah!" She smiled, grasped my hand again, then stood up, ruffled my hair, and went into the kitchen.

I looked after her, shaking my head involuntarily. Why was she so personal and intimate to a stranger? What did she *want*?

This case is a good example of poor communication due to cultural differences in conventions and body language. Greece is a collectivist culture, with much emphasis on the extended family. Mrs. Theodoridis is treating Ray like a family member because of his close relationship to her son—indeed she is treating him as if he *is* her son. And like many people in Southern Europe, Greek people have a low interpersonal distance, and touching of the type Mrs. Theodoridis is doing is not uncommon, particularly between members of the extended family. But Ray, from the more reserved, higher-distance Australian culture, sees all this as intrusive; in his culture, touching between men and women often has sexual connotations. No wonder he is confused! In failing to notice Ray's embarrassment Mrs. Theodoridis shows low cultural intelligence.

The topic of body language is popular, and most of us now realize that we communicate, often inadvertently, by such means as physical proximity and orientation to another person, body movements, gestures, facial expression, eye contact, and tone of voice. Thus, nonverbal communication supplements verbal communication.

Often, nonverbal communication is a good guide to the truth; for example, if athletes are sitting in the dressing room after the match with shoulders slumped, arms folded, and faces glum, you do not need to ask, whatever their culture, whether their team won or lost. Sometimes nonverbal behavior reveals the opposite of verbal, for example, when someone making a visible effort to control himself, shouts, "No, I'm *not* angry!"

However, many nonverbal signals are similar between different cultures. For example, smiling universally expresses positive feelings. But there are also subtle variations. Asians often smile to conceal nervousness or embarrassment. Shaking the head means disagreement in Western cultures but agreement in some parts of India. The codes that tell us the meanings of postures or gestures, or where to stand or whether to bow, sometimes agree across cultures but sometimes disagree.

DISTANCE

How close should you stand when communicating with others? Should you face them directly? The answer can vary according to the characteristics of the other person, for example, their authority, age, or gender. But there are also cultural differences. For example, in casual conversation,

Greeks stand closer than Americans, who stand closer than Norwegians. A culturally intelligent person will be mindful of the comfort of others and will modify his or her social distance.[12]

TOUCHING

Should you ever touch the other person? If so, where, and how much? Who can touch whom, and on what part of the body, is explicit in most cultures. Touching another person symbolizes various emotions and relationships. The most obvious example is the handshake, which in many cultures denotes a friendly relationship—"I'm pleased to meet you" or "Goodbye for now." In France, kissing another person's cheek is common between men as well as women. In some cultures, approval or support is shown by a slap on the back or a squeeze of the arm.

There are low-touch cultures (predominantly in North America, Northern Europe, and Asia) and high-touch cultures (predominantly in Latin America, Southern and Eastern Europe, and the Middle East). A touch that is meant to be meaningful in the United States, such as a pat on the back, might not even be noticed in a high-touch culture like Brazil. Because of the sexual connotations of touching, conventions are often different for men and women.

BODY POSITION

In a case in Chapter 1, a Samoan job applicant showed respect by positioning himself at a physically lower level than the HR manager, but the gesture misfired because to Americans sitting down when others are standing shows *dis*respect. Polite Americans wait for others to sit down first, and show respect by rising from their seats when others enter the room. The way people position themselves has meaning in all cultures, but there are no hard-and-fast rules.

Another common body-position issue is the adoption of a particular body shape—for example a rigid, angular stance denoting aggression or a curled-up, cowering posture indicating submissiveness.[13] Bowing to show deference is common, but in some cultures its use is extreme. In Japan, the (unwritten) rules about who should bow to whom and how they should do it are complex, subtle, and difficult to master. Indeed, foreigners attempting Japanese bowing are at best humorous and at worst offensive, making bowing in Japan a custom best reserved for native Japanese.

GESTURES

Hand and arm movements are often used as physical accompaniments to words, to supplement them or to provide a visual illustration. Often gestures are meaningless without the verbal commentary, other than as a general statement of the person's state of mind. But other gestures have established meanings, including pointing to indicate direction, hands held up with the palms facing upward and outward to indicate defensiveness, and a shrug of the shoulders to indicate incomprehension or lack of interest. Other signals vary across cultures. Some gestures (for example, the thumbs-up sign) are positive, humorous, or harmless in some cultures but are considered hostile, offensive, or obscene in others. High-CQ people tend to avoid explicit gestures until they know exactly what they mean.

FACIAL EXPRESSION

Facial expressions indicate the basic human emotions: happiness: surprise, disgust, fear, anger, and sadness. These facial expressions are instinctive and common.[14] However, in many cultures people have learned how to disguise their emotions by adopting an expression that does not represent how they really feel. For example, is the flight attendant beaming happily at every passenger truly happy to meet each one? In some Asian cultures, smiling is often used to hide displeasure, sadness, or anger.

Emotions can also be concealed behind a neutral expression. Every negotiator and card player knows the value of being able to sit with a face devoid of expression. Thus, while natural facial expressions provide a cross-cultural *code* to others' emotions, *conventions* can mean that facial cues are either absent or misleading. In collectivist cultures, the open expression of individual emotion is often suppressed because it may threaten group harmony. This is one reason for Westerners characterizing Chinese and Japanese people as inscrutable.

EYE CONTACT

Making, or avoiding, eye contact is another form of non-verbal communication. In Western countries moderate eye contact during conversation communicates friendliness or interest, whereas excessive eye contact (staring) is considered rude, and lack of eye contact as hostile. Eye contact can also be used as a signal: for example, making eye contact with the other person as you finish a sentence often means "Now it's your turn to speak." But Arabs, Latinos, Indians, and Pakistanis all have conventions of longer eye contact, whereas Africans and East Asians interpret eye contact as conveying anger or insubordination. Also, most cultures have different conventions about eye contact depending on the gender, status, and so on of those involved.

In all areas of nonverbal communication, the ability to observe the behavior of others, to be mindful of it, and to be skilled at modifying one's own behavior are key components of cultural intelligence.

Negotiating across Cultures

In negotiation the objective is to overcome sometimes conflicting interests and reach an agreement that is advantageous to all. The tools of negotiation include threats and promises, persuasion, the signaling of concessions, and the development of compromises and creative solutions. Again, cross-cultural differences cause complications. Most international tourists know, for example, that in some countries it is accepted custom to haggle in shops, while in others one is expected to pay the marked price.

WHEN IS IT TIME TO DO BUSINESS?

Bill Miller, an American salesman with a major IT company, sits in his Mexico City hotel room, head bowed, feeling totally frustrated. Two days into his trip and with only tomorrow left, he feels as far from closing the sale he is trying to make as he was when he arrived.

It's not that his Mexican hosts are hostile. They smile broadly at him, take a personal interest in him, and certainly look after all his physical needs: the hotel, for example, is excellent. But they show little interest in talking business. The manager who has been assigned to look after Bill is a good host but is not party to the deal Bill wants to negotiate. On the first day, when Bill talked about his prepared sales presentation, the manager seemed surprised. "Plenty of time for that later," he advised. "Why not relax for a day or two and do some sightseeing first? I can look after you."

So Bill spent his first two days being shown around Mexico City. On the second day, however, his host invited him to an after-work meeting with the senior managers of the company. Bill prepared carefully and arrived promptly at the meeting room with his PowerPoint display. No presentation space or projector was available, and no one was there, only some drinks and nibbles. Gradually the Mexicans drifted in, got themselves drinks, and stood around chatting. They engaged Bill conversationally in English and asked questions. But the questions were not about the equipment Bill wanted to sell but about his company—its history, its plans, and its future expansion in Latin America. And they asked about Bill himself—his history in the company, his view of the industry, even his wife, family, and hobbies.

Bill wanted to get on with his presentation, but he did not want to offend his hosts. Eventually, during a pause, he said, "Thanks—I am grateful for your hospitality. Now, can we sit down and let me go through my presentation. I think we have a good deal here for your company."

There was an embarrassed silence. Then the deputy CEO said slowly, "Unfortunately, I think Mr. Alvarez may already have gone home." Alvarez was the CEO, whose signature to the deal was imperative. "Maybe . . . tomorrow? In the meantime, why not come out to dinner so we can get to know each other better?" This time, Bill pleaded fatigue.

How on earth, he wondered, did these people ever sell anything to each other or buy anything from each other, let alone from him?

Back at his home, Juan Alvarez lit a cigarette thoughtfully. The American had looked so ill at ease that Juan just hadn't felt like sticking around. He had wanted to try to build a long-term business relationship, but Miller didn't seem interested. Alvarez had seen it before with Americans.

How on earth, he wondered, did these people ever learn to really trust each other in business?

The reflections of Miller and Alvarez reveal different outlooks on business relationships. Bill, like most Americans, is concerned with the short-term, with reaching a conclusion and not wasting time on social trivia. Juan and his staff, like members of most Latin cultures and many others, believe that good business is the result of good relationships. Therefore, the initial effort must go into building a relationship: it is worth spending time to do so.

The result is that both Bill and Juan endanger what they value most—Bill endangers the immediate transaction, and Juan endangers the long-term business relationship. If each (or even either) had been willing to accommodate, at least in part, the other's customs, a worthwhile business relationship could by now be under way and each could secure exactly what he wants.

Negotiating Styles

Negotiation processes typically go through different phases:

- building a relationship
- exchanging information
- trying to persuade each other
- making concessions and reaching agreement[15]

There are cultural differences in the emphasis on each phase. Generally, people in Western cultures take a relatively transactional approach to negotiation, focusing mainly on the last two stages. Many other cultures focus on creating a background relationship and emphasize the social side of the situation. In this case, Bill Miller and Juan Alvarez couldn't negotiate with each other because each was stuck in a different part of the process. Culturally intelligent Americans learn to be sociable and patient in negotiation, and culturally intelligent Asians and Latinos learn to get to the point more quickly.

Styles of persuasion may also differ. In Western societies, rational argument is favored, whereas in some other countries, appeals to emotion or ideology may be used. Western negotiators, having individualist values, have a competitive negotiating style, whereas Asians tend to be more polite, more obscure, and more restrained.

A key cultural variable in negotiation is power distance (see Chapter 2), the extent to which people expect to see power and authority invoked to solve problems. The arbitration model of negotiation supposes that whenever differences of interest have to be negotiated, there should be a higher-level authority figure making decisions and imposing it on all parties. This is often observed in Japan. Another model is the bureaucratic one, which attempts to reduce the need for negotiation by specifying in advance rules and procedures for solving disagreements. This model is often observed in Germany.

There are also differences in the details of negotiating: for example, the level at which initial offers are made and the willingness of negotiators to make concessions. An American negotiator might be surprised by a Chinese, Arab, or Russian counterpart because these groups often start off with extreme positions. Russians are also reluctant to make concessions, seeing this as a sign of weakness, whereas other groups, such as North Americans and Arabs, will make concessions and respond to others' concessions. Finally, of course, the generalizations made above are subject to substantial individual differences.

One way of thinking about the negotiation process is in terms of metaphors. The very different culturally based metaphors of sports and households can explain American and Japanese negotiations. Individualist Americans are task-oriented, accept conflict as normal, and try to conduct an orderly process with rules within which they have the chance to excel and win, much in the same way that athletes do. The household symbolizes the more collectivist Japanese, who, in contrast, are focused on relationships, want to avoid conflict and save face, and get satisfaction from performing their roles rather than from winning.[16] Understanding your own negotiation metaphor and the culturally based metaphors of others can give you insight into how to achieve a mutually satisfactory outcome.

Principles for Cross-Cultural Communication and Negotiation

There is plenty of information available on cross-cultural communication and negotiation, from both everyday observation and systematic research, but spelling out hard-and-fast rules is difficult. However, here are some broad principles.

- *Gain the knowledge to anticipate differences.* Learn about the codes and conventions of groups you deal with. Be aware of the various areas of difference we have noted in this chapter—for example, verbal versus nonverbal, contextual versus non-contextual, different negotiating styles. Learn the prevailing cultural values of the country—for example, individualist versus collectivist—and think about how these may influence the process. What might be their metaphor for negotiation?

- *Practice mindfulness.* Pay attention not just to the code and content of messages but also to the context and the conventions of communication. By attending to *how* messages are delivered you can acquire additional information. Question attributions. In Chapter 3 we discussed how we can go behind the surface behavior of others to attribute motivation and meaning. As we have seen, the meaning we usually attribute is based on a familiar understanding of our own behavior and that of our cultural group. Practicing mindfulness helps us to see new possibilities of meanings in the behavior of other cultural groups.

- *Develop cross-cultural skills.* How much should you adapt your behavior to accommodate the codes, conventions, and style of another culture? Should you try to imitate them or just be yourself? Some adaptation seems to improve relationships by making the other party more comfortable, but too much adaptation can cause suspicion and distrust. Finding the optimal point of adaptation is an art. By improving your cultural intelligence, you can gain a repertoire of adaptive skills and the knowledge of when they are appropriate.

Summary

Communication is fundamental to social interactions and relationships. Because of differences in background, codes, or conventions, cross-cultural communication faces many barriers to shared understanding. Language skills are important, but cross-cultural communication involves additional abilities. Culturally based codes and conventions also involve nonverbal signals and communication styles. Negotiation is a special communication situation involving conflicting goals. While all negotiations follow a similar process, the emphasis placed on each stage varies across cultures. The challenging nature of negotiations makes high cultural intelligence a prerequisite for knowing when, how, and how much to adapt one's behavior to achieve the most successful outcome.

CHAPTER **6**

Motivating and Leading across Cultures

CLASS CONDUCT

Kenichi Tokuzawa, a Japanese man of twenty-four, was a graduate in languages and was fluent in various languages, including English. Prior to his university study, he had trained as a schoolteacher, had taught for two years in a Japanese primary school, and had been acclaimed as an outstanding teacher. Kenichi put his success down to his clear structuring of lessons, meticulous preparation, effective use of language, and ability to make topics interesting. The results were impressive: when Kenichi taught, every student paid close attention.

In his final year at university, Kenichi won an international scholarship enabling him to spend a semester studying at a university in New England, including the opportunity to teach at a local school, conducting daily classes in conversational Japanese with a tenth-grade class.

Kenichi realized it would be a challenge to teach students from another culture who were older than those he had taught before but believed his thorough preparation and proven teaching techniques could transcend cultural boundaries. He had heard that American students take a more relaxed approach to their studies and expect to participate more in class than do Japanese, but as a young Japanese well educated in U.S. culture, he thought he would be able to get on the same wavelength as American teenagers.

On his first day in his new class, Kenichi, immaculately dressed, walked to the front of the classroom, bowed, smiled, and said, "Good morning. I am Mr. Tokuzawa. I am here to teach you Japanese." A few girls tittered, and several boys continued to talk among themselves. A little rattled, Kenichi tapped the desk loudly with his pen. "Please listen to me," he said, more loudly, and repeated his greeting. This time there was more attention but also further suppressed giggles. A youth at the back of the class rolled his eyes toward the ceiling.

Recognizing the possibility of a challenge to his authority, Kenichi decided to impose it. Briskly, he asked a student to distribute his meticulous course notes. Clearly and methodically, he explained the syllabus and grading system. He asked if there were any questions. There were none. Rather than being eager to participate, the students seemed bored, listless. It was the same when he started teaching. He followed the schedule he had carefully prepared. He asked the students to repeat his words back and to translate, and a few did so. But they did so unwillingly, as if they were answering his questions only to break the silence. The atmosphere at the front of the class was leaden. At the back the students were restless. The boy who had rolled his eyes put his head down on his desk, apparently asleep.

Dismissing the students at the end of the class, Kenichi overheard a girl remark to her friend, "Is that guy uptight! He ought to chill out." Chill out? He didn't know the expression. But he did realize that his class had been a major step backward. The class was just not in a mood to listen, to learn, to be led by him. Why? Were they not interested in the subject? Were these simply the norms of the school, or the United States? Or was there something he himself had simply gotten wrong?

In this case, Kenichi's problem is one of *leadership*. Leadership has been defined as "the ability to influence other people to strive willingly to reach common goals."[1] As well as being the teacher of the class, he is its leader. It is his job to influence the students to "strive willingly" toward the common goal of learning.

Why has he not succeeded? While we can't say for sure, it seems likely that his style of leadership was too Japanese to fit with the culture and expectations of his American students. Japanese have higher power distance (see Chapter 2) than Americans; that is, they expect a leader to exercise authority as a right. In Japan leaders are respected because of their positions, whereas in the United States they must earn respect through their actions. In Japan, respect is shown partly by *not* participating, that is, by respecting what the leader says and does and not speaking until the leader invites you to do so. Japanese schoolchildren are therefore respectful of their teachers and ready to pay attention and accept the teacher's instructions. The Americans in Kenichi's class might have responded better if he had been less formal and had found out more about them—by being mindful—before launching into his own agenda. Kenichi may find it difficult to get his students to be receptive. Can Kenichi motivate this class? Is he a leader?

Motivation across Cultures

In order to lead, one must understand the motivation of those being led—their willingness to exert effort toward a goal. Patterns of motivation vary both between individuals and across cultures. For example, achievement motivation (striving for individual success) is higher in individualist cultures, and affiliation motivation (seeking good interpersonal relationships) is higher in collectivist cultures, but in both cases there may be exceptions.

It is the leader's task to provide rewards appropriate to the cultural and individual characteristics of the situation. This task requires leaders to understand the motives of their followers, how these can be mobilized, and how effective action can be rewarded. An important aspect of motivation is individuals' attitudes to the allocation of rewards, particularly the issue of equity (fair distribution of rewards) versus equality (equal distribution of rewards). Preference for equity (which leads to more unequal rewards) over equality tends to be related to power distance. Collectivist societies prefer more equally distributed rewards, whereas individualist societies believe that individual performance should be rewarded with benefits related to the level of performance of the individual.

Popular Ideas of Leadership

There is much public confusion about leadership. Many people believe in the "Great Man" theory of leadership and have people in mind who personify leadership to them—such as Gandhi, John F. Kennedy, Joan of Arc, or Sun Tzu. We think of such people as having the "gift" of leadership and being able to lead effectively regardless of situation, task, or culture. However, leading across cultures raises questions:

- What made these people leaders and others not?
- Would these people have been great leaders at another time, in another place, with different followers, or in another culture?

A parallel to the Great Man theory is the "One Best Way" theory. Some people believe that there is a set of definable practices that will inevitably bring success in leadership.

Leadership would be easier if either theory were true. Unfortunately both are plain wrong.[2] Many people—both men and women—can be effective leaders in different situations and cultures, and those effective in one situation will not necessarily be so in another. Likewise, effective leaders influence their followers in different ways. A leader may capture the loyalty of some followers while being rejected and ridiculed by others. A style that works perfectly in one situation (such as with construction workers in Dubai) may fall flat in another (such as with software engineers in Silicon Valley).

Even within cultures, leaders need to display the mindfulness and adaptability skills discussed in Chapter 3 just to understand the special features of the situation and vary their leadership to fit the amount of power at their disposal, the characteristics of their followers, and the tasks to be accomplished. Becoming a culturally intelligent leader is a major challenge. Yet as more and more leaders find themselves, as Kenichi Tokuzawa did, dealing with followers who are culturally different from themselves (and often culturally different from each other) or leading in settings with different traditions and expectations for leadership, a culturally intelligent approach is vital.

Leadership Styles

Our understanding of culturally intelligent leadership begins with a look at leadership styles—a concept based on research conducted in the United States that has been assumed to be valid, and has often been applied, elsewhere. These studies attempted to relate organizational performance—as indicated by measures such as productivity, quality, and staff morale— to different styles of leadership behavior. Two dimensions that have shown up consistently are *concern for tasks* (getting things done) and *concern for relationships* (getting along well with people). Research indicates that relationship-oriented leaders tend to have more satisfied subordinates, and that this is true across a range of different cultures.[3]

However, most organizations are at least as interested in employees' performance as in their satisfaction, and the evidence on the relationship of leadership style to performance is more complex. Task-oriented leadership, for example, can take different forms—such as detailed goal-directed planning or autocratic command. People from different cultures react to task-oriented leadership in different and often unpredictable ways. There are also numerous other factors, such as the structure of the task, the power of the leader, and the behavior of subordinates—who, of course, are frequently themselves trying to influence the leader—so that statements about leadership must often be hedged with the statement "it depends." In short, researchers have not found one best way of leadership that works across all cultures. In the next section, examples of leadership from around the world are provided so that we can begin to understand the enormous complexity and subtlety of the cultural forces affecting leadership.

Leadership around the World

THE ARAB WORLD

Leadership in Arab societies demonstrates how history and culture can influence the traditions, practices, and expectations of leadership. Islamic religion and tribal traditions have always been strong and remain so, but Arabic countries are now touched by Western culture. Islam tends to think of leadership as a job for men. Tribal traditions oblige leaders to behave like fathers, protecting and nurturing followers (employees) as they would their children, and to take responsibility for the whole enterprise. Overlaying this system is bureaucracy, historically introduced by the Ottoman Empire and continued by Europeans in the twentieth century as a way of keeping control of their businesses and other institutions.

The resultant leadership style, which has been termed *sheikhocracy*,[4] involves personal autocracy and conformity to rules and regulations based not on the rules' rationality, but on respect for those who made them. This means that rules have symbolic importance but will not be implemented if they go against autocratic tribal traditions. For example, the rules may specify procedures for appointment on merit, but these are likely to be ignored in favor of appointments based on family relationships and friendships.

In Japan, a key factor influencing leadership is the cultural value of *amae,* meaning (loosely translated) *indulgent love,* the kind that parents have for their children. Whereas in some societies, children are taught to be independent of their parents, in Japan, *amae* affects all relationships, including manager-subordinate relationships. Japanese managers therefore tend to take a deep interest in employees' personal lives. Subordinates often ask superiors for advice, including advice on personal matters such as choice of a spouse.

Amae in Japanese relationships also gives rise to other relevant cultural norms. Leader behavior is embedded in a network of reciprocal obligations (*on* and *giri*). *On* is a debt or obligation, and *giri* is the moral obligation to repay the debt, and every action creates both. A leader who neglects the obligation to reciprocate will lose followers' trust and support. A Japanese leader's effectiveness is thus based largely on the ability to understand and attract followers.[5]

THE OVERSEAS CHINESE

The leadership style of ethnic Chinese living outside mainland China reflects their modern organizations but is entrenched in Chinese culture and tradition, where a leader's legitimacy is based on loyalty to the patriarch. Similarly, the word of the founder or CEO of modern Chinese organizations is law, and his authority resembles that of a head of the household. All the key people in the organization are related to the founder, and to each other, by blood or marriage, enabling the overseas Chinese to run their modern corporations as family businesses. Mutual trust among family members—basing decisions on what is best for the clan—underlies all leader-follower relationships.[6]

FRANCE

Leadership in France is heavily influenced by the strong societal emphasis on hierarchy. At the top of French organizations is the CEO, who will have attended the "right" university, one of the "Grandes Écoles." The style of these top managers is often paternalistic and charismatic in the style of the great field marshals of France.[7] Between the top managers and the workers is a large group of middle managers or *cadres*, who deal with multiple rules and regulations. While seeming bewilderingly inefficient to the outsider, these organizations operate very reliably.

RUSSIA

The image of Russian leaders as powerful autocrats is based on the country's long history of centralized authority and responsibility.[8] In medieval Russia, village elders were entrusted to represent the common will of the people, and suggestions and criticisms were never credited to any one individual. It was the elders' task to sort through the comments: their decisions went unchallenged and they bore full responsibility for the group's welfare. Later, under state socialism, these same traditional attitudes were evident in communist organizations. Although advised by workers' councils, the heads of enterprises wielded all the power and bore all the responsibility.

This centralization of power resulted in a top-heavy bureaucracy that some suggest was the fatal flaw in the socialist system. When things went wrong, as they often did, no one would take action without authorization from a superior. As Russian firms try to find their way in their new free-market environment, managers now struggle to push responsibility down the hierarchy and to delegate routine tasks. Consider the following case:

MANAGEMENT BY OBJECTIVES IN RUSSIA

Dahl Ekelund, a Norwegian with a good track record as a leader in various European engineering enterprises, has been appointed executive director of the Russian subsidiary of Motor Corporation. The directors want him to release some of the potential in a workforce that is well qualified, talented, and experienced, but knows little about modern management.

In his first week in his new job, Dahl conducts a seminar to introduce the concept of Management by Objectives (MBO)[9] to his managers. He is amazed by the hostility directed not only at his message but also at himself. When he suggests that all employees should write their own objectives, his subordinates came out with comments such as: "We have lived without this kind of thing for some years and have made great strides. We don't need a new bureaucracy."

Dahl explains how MBO provides new opportunities for staff involvement and participation. The managers retort that others have tried to implement Western managerial methods in the company—nobody has succeeded. Irritated, Dahl answers brusquely, "Everybody working here is going to be using these modern methods. I expect a written outline from each of you of your next year's goals within two weeks. And get the same information from your subordinates within three weeks. And for those who don't—no bonus. That will be all."

As he leaves, Dahl overhears the comments:

"Well, now, Petrovich, you'll be writing goals rather than working."

"Never, let him do it himself."

"But, what about losing your bonus?"

"Yeah, we'll see."[10]

In this case, the leadership expectations of the Russians are shaped by both Russian culture and years of working in organizations still influenced by the remnants of state socialism. These Russian middle managers demonstrate an expectation for autocratic leadership and have great difficulty accepting, or trusting, their own participation or that of their subordinates in setting goals. Their reluctance is made worse by skepticism about their superior's concern for, or control over, their futures. Under state socialism each autocratic boss was someone else's puppet. Their beliefs persist long after the demise of the socialist policies that created them.

In seeking to help the company modernize, a higher-CQ Dahl Ekelund might have applied cultural intelligence by

- avoiding the *Be Like Me* approach to management that he had learned in his cultural background in Western Europe (*knowledge*)
- taking time to learn some of the special characteristics of the new culture that he was entering (*knowledge*)
- spending time observing and talking to his new subordinates for a few weeks after arrival, trying to understand their collective and individual areas of comfort and discomfort before trying to institute change (*mindfulness*)
- trying to understand from the Russian perspective why they might be acting the way they were (*mindfulness*)
- listening to what his staff is saying (and being aware of what they are not saying) rather than becoming irritated and closing the meeting abruptly (*mindfulness* and *adaptive behavior*)
- introducing a less ambitious form of MBO, for example, having leaders set goals for their subordinates, then making a gradual move toward participative methods (*adaptive behavior*)

These examples from different countries show the complexity of the cultural forces affecting leadership. Note the importance of historical factors and tradition, and the acceptance, under the right circumstances, of apparently autocratic leadership. Individuals with high cultural intelligence are mindfully attentive to such factors and work hard to develop the cross-cultural skills to be effective. An international manager known to one of the authors, whose job took him into leadership roles all around the globe, would voraciously read books on the history and customs of the countries he was due to visit in order to acquire background knowledge and sensitivity to the local situation. However, such knowledge is only the starting place for becoming a culturally intelligent leader. One of the most culturally intelligent leaders in business today may be Carlos Ghosn, CEO of the Renault-Nissan Alliance. Ghosn was born in Brazil to Lebanese parents and was educated in France. He is credited with turning around the fortunes of Nissan in Japan, a country he knew little about before going there. He attributes his success to his multicultural background, which gave him what we would call cultural intelligence.[11]

Culture and Expectations of Followers

Culturally intelligent leadership involves focusing on followers. In some ways the idea of leadership is an invention of those who want to be in charge or who believe that their traditional or hierarchical position entitles them to be in charge. But in a sense, everyone is in charge; everyone has the potential to exercise leadership. We have defined leadership in terms of influence, and influence may be exercised by anyone, from the highest to the lowest member of an organization. In understanding how leadership works across cultures, we need to look at all participants—how they might understand a situation, whether they might expect a leader to tell them what to do, or whether and how they might exercise influence in their own right. Thus, even lower-level members of an organization working within their own culture may offer cultural understanding in a leadership process.

The designated leader needs to think not just about how he or she might exercise influence but about how that influence might usefully interact with the influence exercised by others. For example, a culturally intelligent Dahl Ekelund could use local formal and informal cultural processes to find out and consider the views of his subordinates before setting goals for them exactly as they want him to.

Here, it is useful to recap the key values dimensions outlined in Chapter 2.

- In individualist cultures, people are concerned about themselves, prefer activities to be conducted privately, and expect decisions to be made by the individual according to his or her judgment and the anticipated rewards.

- In collectivist cultures, people view themselves as members of groups and collectives, prefer group activities, and expect decisions to be made on a consensual or consultative basis, where the effects of the decision on everyone are taken into account.

In such cultures, two very different styles of leadership would be expected. Western countries tend to be individualist, so both leaders and followers attempt to involve themselves in influence processes to maximize their individual influence and get themselves a good result. Higher management frequently tries to utilize individualism to its advantage by offering leaders individual rewards for the accomplishments of the group or by holding the leader accountable for its performance. Collectivist societies rely more on the leader to involve the group—a shared expectation of both leader and group members.

Other cultural forces influence the expectations of leaders. Some cultures value formality and expect leaders to honor ceremonies and observances. In cultures where punctuality is important, there will be pressure on leaders to turn up on time, and in future-oriented societies, to focus on long-term strategy. Because of the special status of the position, the leader is often the most led member of the group—led, that is, by the cultural context.

In many societies, historical and cultural forces—such as high power distance, Confucianism, and feudalism—practices and expectations of leadership have developed that are best described as *paternalistic*.[12] Paternalism (literally "being fatherly") involves creating a family atmosphere, having close relationships with followers to the extent of getting involved in their non-work lives, and expecting both deference and loyalty. Paternalism often leads to positive employee attitudes, and some Western organizations have tried to use paternalism as a means of having a contented, compliant workforce. In the wrong culture, though, such efforts can backfire.[13]

Leading in Multinational Organizations

Leading any culturally diverse organization or group requires cultural intelligence. But in large multinational organizations with subsidiaries in many countries, the problem is increased. Typically there are organizational requirements for central control and uniformity to ensure that the organization remains stable and that subsidiaries work toward a common goal. But when such organizations attempt to manage their own diverse communities of people in a uniform manner, major problems emerge, as the following case shows.

THE COMMON BOND

Jenny Gendall is a secretary employed by the New Zealand office of Technica, a U.S.-based multinational organization, which has offices in over seventy countries.[14] In response to the cultural diversity of its multinational workforce, Technica has implemented many new policies and procedures, including a nondiscrimination policy for employment procedures.

Technica's head office in the United States has recently developed a set of values designed to provide a framework that all Technica employees will use in their day-to-day actions. The values reflect Technica's "critical success factors" and will offer shared values to all employees, thereby making Technica a better place to work. The statement of values is known as Our Common Bond, and a key value is respect for the individual: "We treat each other with respect and dignity, valuing individual and cultural differences. We communicate frequently and with candor, listening to each other regardless of level or position."

Technica's head office has disseminated an action plan for

implementing Our Common Bond. To ensure conformity, each subsidiary, including New Zealand, has received directives, manuals, training programs, videos, and visits by international facilitators. To Jenny Gendall, who considers that the New Zealand office has always been a good place to work in terms of respect, valuing equity, and all the rest of it, it seems like a lot of fuss about nothing.

Indeed, Jenny notes that some of her colleagues are beginning to question the values, the language used, and the method of implementation. The values are being imposed without discussion, are in "American language," and are inappropriate within New Zealand. According to Jenny, "The Common Bond is just about day-to-day courtesy. It doesn't need to be spelled out. Why was it forced on the entire company? I hate that airy-fairy, warm-fuzzy stuff. I just want to get on with the job. We're free and easy over here, and the Common Bond just doesn't suit our Kiwi style. And we're all different. The Common Bond says we need to 'listen to each other regardless of level or position,' but some of our Maori and Pacific Island employees still expect to show, and be shown, proper respect for status."

In this case, Technica seeks to establish a corporate culture that will encompass all its international subsidiaries. But its "universal" values cannot easily be translated across cultural boundaries, even between apparently similar cultures like the United States and New Zealand, as the values may act as a touchstone for contradiction and cultural conflict. Although Technica is genuinely international and culturally diverse, a definite "home" culture still emanates from the U.S. head office; and, notwithstanding its talk of embracing diversity, in its global leadership and recognition of other cultures, Technica is not truly "walking the walk." The effect, at least in New Zealand, is that instead of embracing diversity, employees tend to criticize, ignore, and subvert the changes.

"Managing diversity" is a positive goal for multinationals, but the means of achieving it need to be locally specific and probably locally devised. In international organizations a useful guide for managing diversity is the simple notion of "think global and act local."

Also important in this case is the question, who is the leader? There is a difference between formal leadership (with a formally appointed leader who has an appropriate job title) and informal leadership (in which someone has leadership status because of the respect of others). Informal leaders arise because their ideas or behavior are well received by others and because of their good communication skills. Thus, in the case above, informal leaders in New Zealand may subvert the leadership of formal bosses in the United States. Ideally, the formal and informal leaders are the same person, but in a cross-cultural situation a formal leader from another culture may not be accepted because of cultural differences, particularly in expected methods of leadership, and an informal leader from the home culture representing the ideas of local employees may exercise countervailing influence. Formal leaders may therefore have to either exercise a leadership style that fits local expectations or be able to work with the informal leader.

Different cultures also have different prototypes of what a leader should be like. A leader who is able to meet followers' expectations of a good leader can develop better trust and relationships.

Followership

From the foregoing, it is evident that anyone in a group, and not just the formal boss, has the potential to be a leader. In most groups, leadership is at least partially shared. Further, the exercise of leadership implies a duty of followers to follow. Therefore, in multicultural groups and organizations, becoming culturally intelligent is an advantage to the follower as well to the leader. Being able to read one's formal leader and colleagues, taking into account their national culture, is an advantage. Cultural intelligence is for everyone!

The Common Thread: Charismatic or Transformational Leadership

An idea that has dominated recent thinking about leadership is transformational leadership, which influences people to go beyond their own immediate interests and objectives and to work hard to achieve performance beyond expectations.[15] To do this, the leader has to present a compelling vision of the future and inspire followers by demonstrating or modeling the behavior desired from followers. S/he must stimulate and challenge followers and show each one individual consideration. All of these tasks are easier if the leader has the cultural knowledge and mindfulness characteristic of high CQ.

Perhaps the easiest way to understand transformational leadership is to think of well-known leaders such as Winston Churchill, John F. Kennedy, and Martin Luther King Jr. However, Eastern leaders such as the Indian political and spiritual leader Mahatma Gandhi also meet the criteria for a transformational leader, as does the great South African leader Nelson Mandela, even though they practiced it in a very different way, one that was in tune with the expectations and cultural values of their followers. Note the cultural variety of these examples. A leader with high cultural intelligence will be able to provide a vision, engage others' motivation, and model behavior in ways consistent with the culture and values of followers.

There is research that supports the effectiveness of transformational leadership across a range of different countries.[16] Yet people from different countries expect transformational leaders to behave very differently. Having a vision and engaging others may require very different behavior in different cultures. For example, being seen to have suffered might be important in Japan, while being seen as decisive would carry more weight in the United States.

Culturally Intelligent Leadership

Making sense of leadership is difficult enough, even without the complication of cultural differences. While there is no universally effective prescription for leading culturally diverse followers, there are some things we can say for certain that culturally intelligent leaders know and do.

- Leadership is largely in the minds of followers. If followers perceive a person as a leader, he or she will gain the power, authority, and respect afforded a leader.

- Followers expect leaders to have (a) a vision for the group or organization, (b) the ability to communicate this vision clearly, and (c) skill in organizing followers toward the vision. However, the behavior that indicates these characteristics differs among cultures.

- The leadership dimensions of task orientation and relationship orientation exist in every culture, but the behaviors that indicate these orientations are specific to different cultures.

- Some followers need more leading along each of these dimensions than others. Factors such as organizational norms and the education levels of followers can act as substitutes for leadership. For example, a group of research scientists typically needs very little task orientation from their leader: they already know what to do.

- Trying to mimic the behaviors of a leader belonging to the followers' culture may lead to unintended consequences. Some adoption of these behaviors will gain a leader acceptance by followers, but too much may be interpreted as insincere or even offensive.[17]

In summary, if you want to be a culturally intelligent leader, you will need to use knowledge and mindfulness to develop a repertoire of behaviors that can be adapted to specific situations. Doing so involves knowledge of the likely expectations of culturally diverse followers based on generalizations from cultural values such as individualism and collectivism. Through mindful observation, you will gradually refine these expectations. You will also need knowledge of your own preferred style of leadership. What balance of task and relationship orientation feels normal to you? Will you have to work harder at being a relational leader if the situation calls for it? You will also need knowledge of the relevant organizational norms. Trying to be a participative boss in a culture that does not value participation can be counterproductive. Here, mindfulness includes paying attention to follower reactions to particular leadership behaviors and adjusting as necessary.

In cross-cultural situations, it is probably best not to model your leader behavior after a leader in the follower culture. You may look silly trying to behave like Sun Tzu (especially if you are not Chinese) and may find that follower expectations of indigenous leaders may be very different from their expectations of you. Also, in multicultural groups followers can have very different expectations. Therefore, a better role model is a leader like you (e.g., someone from your own culture) who has been particularly effective with these followers.

The needs of followers are extremely important in determining an individual's perceptions of leadership. A culturally intelligent leader is able to find a leadership style that strikes a balance between his or her normal style, the expectations of followers, and the demands of the situation. This balance may well be imperfect, a work in progress. As with surfing or skiing or cycling, finding this balance is initially difficult but becomes easier and feels more natural over time.

Summary

In this chapter we introduced culturally intelligent leadership. Influencing others toward goals is difficult in itself, and the dynamics of cross-cultural interactions increase the challenge. Our understanding of leadership is influenced by individuals we envision as great leaders, who share an ability to communicate a vision and to organize followers. In addition, the idea that leaders can exhibit a task or relationship leadership style has a universal appeal. However, the variety of behaviors that leaders around the world exhibit raises questions about any universal approach. Understanding followers' expectations is a key element in a culturally intelligent approach to leadership. This, plus an individual's preferred style and the constraints imposed by the situation, provide the three dimensions among which the culturally intelligent leader must find balance. While initially difficult to achieve, this equilibrium becomes easier with the development of the knowledge, mindfulness, and behavioral skills of cultural intelligence.

CHAPTER 7

Working with Multicultural Groups and Teams

PARTICIPATE, AND THAT'S AN ORDER!

Harry is the leader of an advertising agency account team that is developing advertising campaigns for a range of clients. The four team members are from different cultural backgrounds and seem to be at odds with each other.

Harry, an American, is clear what the campaigns should be like; he talks about them a lot and tries to persuade his colleagues. But Harry also recognizes the value of diversity, of different ideas. He tells his colleagues that he *welcomes* alternative ideas. He would be delighted for them to suggest ideas that were better than his. Harry says frequently, "Four heads are better than one." His three team members eye each other cautiously.

The only person who responds to Harry's invitations is Ingrid, a recent immigrant from Germany. Unfortunately Ingrid's ideas are not only different from Harry's but also completely opposite. Furthermore, with twenty years' experience in advertising back in Germany, she believes she knows far more than Harry. She therefore backs her ideas vehemently. She too talks, frequently and forcefully. Harry disagrees with her and argues back.

The other two members of the team keep a low profile. José, a Latino, can't stand Ingrid. How *dare* she talk to the boss like that!

117

Has she no respect for authority? It's not so much that José doesn't agree with Ingrid's ideas—in fact he secretly thinks they are quite good; it's the rude and aggressive way she treats Harry that José objects to. So he sides quietly with Harry and wishes Ingrid would go away. He has ideas of his own, of course, but he doesn't believe either Harry or Ingrid would be interested in them.

Ming is a Taiwanese with a demure exterior, and although she is expert in campaign development, she too keeps quiet. Harry says he wants her opinions and ideas, but like José, she doesn't think he means it. Why does he argue so aggressively with Ingrid? If you really want to hear what other people think, Ming believes, you should behave as if you respect them. Listening to Harry and Ingrid makes Ming sad. These people are talented but egocentric. Ming believes good decisions are made through patient reflection, the respectful exchange of ideas, and the protection of the harmony of the group as it works together. So she puts forward her views when Harry asks her, but she speaks so timidly that Harry wonders if Ming herself believes what she is saying.

Many of the differences in the group can be explained by the cultural variation that we introduced in Chapter 2. Westerners such as Harry and Ingrid tend to be high on individualism and autonomy, and moderate or low on power distance and hierarchy. This means that they expect to put forward their own views strongly in groups. Furthermore, they have been brought up and educated to be articulate and persuasive. They tend to believe in creative conflict, in which ideas are pitted against each other until the best one wins. Maybe either Harry will eventually persuade Ingrid, or Ingrid will persuade Harry. But the growing rivalry between the two may make it difficult for either to admit that the other is right.

As for the others, it appears that José has such a high level of power distance, and the associated expectation that decisions should be made by those in authority, that he is unable to accept Ingrid's form of intervention. And Ming appears to be a collectivist who is lost in an individualists' world: she expects modest harmonious discussions in which the goals of the whole group take precedence over individuals' egos. In a group where Ingrid expects the right to challenge, José expects the imposition of authority, and Ming expects a long, courteous decision process, creative discussion seems unlikely.

Each team member explicitly adopts the behavior and the norms learned in his or her culture. Each has brought to this new group his or her own culturally based ideas about how groups should function. They show little mindfulness. In both action and observation, they stick to culturally predetermined scripts.

Yet each of them has much to offer. They all have vital technical expertise. Harry and Ingrid are full of ideas and are articulate in presenting them. Ming has ideals of team harmony and respect for listening, and José recognizes the ultimate need for decisiveness by the leader and group acceptance of decisions. In this case, as in many, diversity of cultural background is not just a problem to be solved; it is an opportunity to be capitalized on. Despite the conflict in the group, its diversity adds huge potential if its members could but see it and harness it.

The Challenge of Teams

Because of the growing diversity of the population, work teams, even in one's home country, are becoming more and more multicultural. This shift presents a dual challenge: how to *contribute* to a multicultural team and how to *manage* a multicultural team.

Once people are organized into teams it also becomes impossible for us to try to handle multiculturalism by dealing with each employee individually according to his or her own cultural needs. We now have to manage not only a set of culturally different individuals but a *process* involving different cultural responses.

An important feature of groups is the difference between *task* and *process* activities.[1] Task activities are directed toward accomplishing the group's goal. Examples include "This is my plan for the advertising campaign..."; "If we do it that way, we will run over budget"; "That's a good suggestion." Process activities are directed at examining and improving how the group goes about this task. Examples of this include "Suppose we go around the group and see what each person thinks"; "I think Jane has something to say, but no one is listening to her"; "We're running short of time, and we'd better have a vote now." Process activities need not be positive: "I'm irritated that you won't tell me what your ideas are"; "When you talk so loudly, I feel intimidated"; "In my country we show respect for other people."

Although groups should spend most of their time dealing with the task at hand, failure to attend to process frequently causes group dysfunction. Groups often become ineffective because their process is overly autocratic or conflicted or indecisive, and they fail to examine what they are doing and change it. When the processes are complicated by culturally different expectations, even more problems can occur.

In the opening case, the successful conclusion of group tasks requires joint problem solving, based on the effective integration of ideas from all members. However, the group's problems are culturally based process problems. The participants all have different models of how the group process should work, but—due in part to the leader's preoccupation with the task and his lack of interest in the process—they have no way of bringing these ideas to the surface or resolving the process issues.

Cultural intelligence helps deal with group development and process issues that are caused or made more difficult by cultural differences. But it can also help solve the process problems associated with any group. High cultural intelligence enables us to observe and understand the different actions and intentions of members, and to acknowledge the cultural diversity of the group and the legitimacy of each member's cultural background. Understanding how members see their roles in the group will improve the quality of their interactions.

By combining this awareness with a focus on getting group processes clear before proceeding to the detail of the task, the team described above could break its impasse and move on to achieving its goals. A culturally intelligent Harry would recognize that his leadership is influenced by his own cultural background and by the individualism and egalitarianism that were part of his makeup and that of his co-worker Ingrid. He would consider how he might accommodate José's and Ming's different characteristics in order to harness their abilities. By attending mindfully to the others' reactions and doing some basic homework on their cultures, he might begin to understand José's deep-seated respect for authority and quiet Ming's hidden talents. By modifying his actions to respect their differences from him, he might gain reciprocal responses, with Ingrid listening more and José and Ming becoming more forthcoming. By explicitly discussing process in team meetings, he might enable all his team members to contribute productively to the group's tasks. Such a process would not only improve task performance, it would also make the team more harmonious and its members more satisfied, and all would improve their cultural intelligence.

Types of Work Groups

Groups are not all the same.[2] One group of workers may have relatively independent jobs but may be in the same workspace or have the same boss. We might call these groups *crews*. Another group may collaborate closely with each other in a process in which the specialist knowledge of each one has to be closely integrated with that of the others. A good name for such groups is *teams*. A third group may be a temporary group expected to solve a specific problem or produce a report or design and then disband. This type of group is often called a *task force*.

These differences involve different ways of working together and therefore affect the cultural aspects of group functioning. Knowing when cultural intelligence matters most can help us to understand why cultural differences have a big effect in some groups and not in others, which will aid in structuring work groups effectively. In crews, group functioning is often predetermined by set procedures and technology, which makes cultural intelligence less important. Task forces, such as the one in our case, might benefit from higher cultural intelligence but may not need to build long-term intercultural relationships. Teams, however, require highly developed trusting long-term relationships between their members, and cultural intelligence and the realization of cross-cultural potential are critical to their effective management.

Group Process and Performance

In both face-to-face and virtual teams, group effectiveness is typically assessed by objective measures of group output, such as production, quality, and sales. However, group morale and cohesiveness, which tend to ensure that performance is maintained over time, are also important. In assessing groups, therefore, wise group leaders consider not just immediate performance but also the processes that the group uses, and the satisfaction and development of group members.

Groups are more than just collections of individuals, and they form their own social processes. Watching an effective team perform can be very exciting; being a member of one, even better. Some teams can, through their own processes, spontaneously create a dynamic of performance or innovation that external influence simply could not prearrange. In particular, in response to the feel-good aspect of working on an interesting problem with others who have different (but complementary) skills and outlooks, workers may release huge unrealized energy or creativity or ideas. It is often exciting to feel the stimulus to thinking that we get from someone who is from a different background, who thinks and talks in a way that is new to us. Different cultures increase the range of viewpoints and approaches available and are therefore a huge potential asset in many group situations. The trick is to create a process that encourages diverse team members and capitalizes on their differences to create this synergy.

On the other hand, groups can develop negative processes that undermine the potential of individual members and reduce group effectiveness. Two common negative processes are groupthink and social loafing.

- In groupthink the group overemphasizes harmony and consensus by killing off dissent and creative alternatives.[3] A famous example was the space shuttle Challenger disaster of 1986, where teams of officials in NASA and the supplying company Morton Thiokol were under intense pressure to ensure that the launch of Challenger was successful and on time. As a result of groupthink, they would not listen to engineers who were telling them that a vital component was likely to fail in cold weather. The launch was authorized in cold conditions, the component failed a minute or two after takeoff, and the spacecraft exploded, killing all on board.

- In social loafing individuals reduce their efforts to complete group tasks in the belief that others in the group will compensate to get the job done.[4] For example, in tug-of-war teams it has been found that as more and more members are added to a team, the average exertion that members apply to the rope decreases.[5] Anyone who has been involved in completing group projects will have noticed at least one person who is not pulling their weight.

It is easy to see how cultural differences such as individualism/collectivism could work for or against such dysfunctional processes.[6] For example, individualists are likely to take a stand against groupthink but are also more likely to take advantage of the group situation by social loafing.

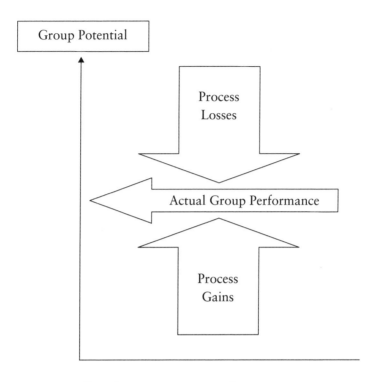

FIGURE 7.1.   Effect of process on group performance

The contribution of process to group effectiveness is the result of both the process losses (such as groupthink and social loafing) and the process gains, or synergies, created in part from the group's diversity. This is shown graphically in Figure 7.1.

A key goal of a multicultural team is therefore to maximize process gains and minimize process losses. This is achieved through cultural synergy (getting the benefits of the cultural differences in the group) and overcoming destructive cultural conflict. The culturally intelligent manager must consider three features of groups through which culture influences their processes. As mentioned previously, the first of these involves the cultural norms and scripts for how groups function that each member brings to a group. The other two are the *cultural diversity* that exists in the group and the *cultural distance* between members.[7]

Cultural Diversity in Groups

A group is diverse—or *heterogeneous*—to the extent that its members are different from each other. Culture is only one dimension on which they are likely to differ; important others are gender, age, and experience.

There is both good and bad news about the effect of diversity in work groups. The bad news is that research has shown that it tends to negatively affect the way members feel about the group.[8] Members of a diverse group are more likely to be dissatisfied with it and less likely to identify with it, which can lead to serious process losses.

Sometimes people respond to this kind of difficulty by deliberately deciding to avoid multicultural groups. This is one reason that countries that accept immigrants from culturally different countries find that despite the immigrants' high qualifications, long experience, and strong work ethic, local organizations often prefer to employ less-qualified local people. Local low-CQ employers tend to think that if they employ immigrants they will suffer major process losses as the newcomers struggle to fit in. In addition, of course, they may simply be prejudiced against them.

To avoid process losses, some organizations have deliberate policies of making groups—particularly production groups—as homogeneous as possible. New Zealand, for example, has a high proportion of Samoan, Tongan, Cook Island, and other Pacific Island workers in the labor force of its cities. Some factories focus on a particular Island community as the basis of their workforces, or try to ensure that work teams are made up of all Samoans or all Tongans. Although proponents of equal employment opportunity may not like such practices, some organizations claim that they ensure there is no ethnic conflict and that each employee feels comfortable with his or her "mates."

This approach is understandable, but it represents a short-term view that does not promote the development of cultural intelligence. The process losses of diversity tend to be immediate, whereas the process gains of diversity take longer to show up. Effort and sensitivity shown in welcoming and orienting people who are culturally different are likely to be rewarded later on, when the process losses disappear and process gains kick in. This is the good-news side of diversity in work groups. Diversity tends to be positively related to group performance in organizational settings, especially when the diversity brings with it task-related skills.

We can understand this by considering what is likely to happen in a totally homogeneous group—that is, a group totally lacking in diversity. Consider a task force trying to solve a technical problem. They are all German. They are all male. They are all graduate engineers. They are all in their fifties. They all studied engineering at the same university, and they are all long-service employees in the same department of the same company. You will probably agree that, competent though they may be, they are unlikely to come up with a range of different ideas.

Diversity provides groups with a wider range of ideas and viewpoints. Like all forms of diversity, diversity in culture encourages diversity in ideas. And the wider the range of ideas, the better the chance of finding good ones. Research shows that cultural diversity often results in more creative and higher-quality group decisions. This comes about not only because of more alternative viewpoints but also because consciousness of cultural difference focuses the group's attention on process issues, including listening to minority viewpoints.[9]

In addition, being culturally different may relate directly to the group's task. In an increasingly globalized world, culturally different group members may possess unique knowledge about culturally different environments. For example, a European or Chinese company planning to export to Brazil or India may recruit Brazilian or Indian members to provide information about relevant cultural or local-market features of their countries.

Cultural Distance in Groups

Another important factor in diverse groups is the *relative cultural distance* of group members. Cultural distance refers to how different each group member feels from each other group member.[10] For example, an Indonesian in a group with an American, a Canadian, and an Australian will feel much more distant than do the other group members, who are culturally similar. When we are very different from the others in a group, it is noticeable to them and to us.

People who are somewhat culturally different from others in their group find it easier than those who are *very* culturally different to become involved in group activities. Overcoming extreme cultural differences may be very difficult. Rather than trying to cross what may seem an unbridgeable gap, some members may withdraw from the group and keep their views to themselves, as happened to José in the Westerner-dominated group in our opening case. If members withdraw, their potential to assist the group is wasted. Group leaders need to decide how to respond to such a situation. For example, should they transfer culturally distant employees to another group where they will feel more at home, or should they try to bridge the cultural gap?

Summarizing research findings about diversity in teams, we can say that diversity provides a team with greater potential for excellence than does homogeneity. But because of the process-loss phenomenon, the risks are also higher that the group will fail.

Culturally Intelligent Group Management

The existence of diversity in a group does not guarantee additional creativity; it merely makes it more possible. The task of the group leader is to facilitate a process that will encourage the creative side of diversity to flourish. Culturally intelligent people can do three things to reduce or eliminate process losses and to capitalize on diversity: (a) manage the environment of the group, (b) allow culturally diverse groups to develop, and (c) foster cultural intelligence in the group.

MANAGING THE GROUP ENVIRONMENT

The functioning of any group depends on its managerial environment: management support, rewards, group status, and opportunities for self-management.

Management Support. Any group requires good management support, such as material resources, relevant information, and psychological support in the form of goodwill and respect. Cross-cultural groups especially need managers who respect cultural difference and appreciate the potential of diversity to improve the organization's creativity and performance. A culturally intelligent team leader attempting to capitalize on cultural diversity is nevertheless likely to fail if external management (particularly senior management) is seen to operate differently.

Rewards. As demonstrated by the case at the beginning of Chapter 4, individualists prefer to be rewarded on the basis of their own contributions. They believe rewards should be equitable. Collectivists often prefer all contributors to the group to be rewarded equally. This sounds like an impossible problem for those who have to decide on reward allocation in a multicultural group. Devising individualized pay systems rewarding each according to preference is impractical, and culturally diverse groups may develop their own consensus about an appropriate balance of individual and group rewards. However, the research on this topic suggests that in any culture, high-performing groups derive a substantial proportion of their rewards from group activities.[11]

Group Status.   Regardless of cultural composition, a group's high status in an organization will increase members' self-esteem. However, the extent to which this is true also depends on cultural differences, particularly the place of the group in the individual's life. In some (primarily collectivist) cultures, the family group is important to the individual above all others, and the work group much less important.

Self-Management.   Providing objectives or general direction for groups—especially for teams—and allowing them to self-manage by finding their own processes is an option that is increasingly fashionable, especially when work is contracted out. Research suggests that self-management has advantages for many teams, cross-cultural or not. For cross-cultural teams, it additionally enables team leaders to develop unique group processes for overcoming the specific cross-cultural issues of the team, without interference from the outside.

DEVELOPMENT OF CULTURALLY
DIVERSE GROUPS

A key element of group development is the selection and allocation of members. Team leaders usually have some discretion—moderated perhaps by legislation or local equal employment opportunity policies—to encourage or discourage diversity as they hire new staff or allocate staff to particular groups. Such decisions need to be carefully considered in relation to cultural issues. For example, are you prepared to accept and manage the likely short-term losses of greater diversity in order to benefit from the prospective longer-term gains?

One option is simply to wait for the group to develop. Research shows that newly formed culturally diverse groups reduce their process losses over time by finding ways of working together better. However, in today's fast-paced world, waiting for this to occur on its own may not be practical. Culturally diverse groups often need feedback about the effectiveness of their processes, feedback that may be best presented from outside the group. Cultural intelligence helps managers strike the right balance between delegation and direction.

DEVELOPING CULTURAL INTELLIGENCE IN THE GROUP

The best way to capitalize on cultural diversity in groups is to ensure that members develop high CQ and that leaders have the will and the skills to explore process issues. Multicultural work groups provide excellent opportunities for members to develop their cultural intelligence. Contact with those who are culturally different can enable group members, by being mindful, to develop their cross-cultural skills. By actively considering the different values, attitudes, and behavior of other members, they can develop their CQ. For this to occur the group must be structured in the following way:[12]

- All members should accept that they have *equal status* within the group (even though status elsewhere may differ).

- To ensure the positive effects of group interaction, the group should be *actively engaged* in a goal-oriented effort.

- The attainment of the common goal must require *interdependent effort* without competition among members.

- Finally, the support of authorities must create a *norm for acceptance* of the group's activities.

In this type of contact, group members gain knowledge about the others who are different, and learn that their knowledge about their co-workers may be wrong or incomplete. Over time they will learn not to generalize about members of this cultural group and will understand and treat them as individuals. Engagement with culturally different people in pursuit of a common goal leads to understanding of the value of different perspectives. Finally, over time, individuals integrate these alternative perceptions into their own thinking. Through recognizing and learning to value differences (by seeing how they can contribute to achieving goals) they confront and reconcile differences in their own minds. By integrating alternative perspectives into their thinking they become more culturally intelligent.

A key element in addressing process issues is providing group members with feedback, which can come from each other and/or from external observers. By understanding the group's dynamics and the causes of its difficulties, members can develop new and more productive ways of changing both their expectations of how the group should function and their own behavior in it.

Virtual Multicultural Groups

A type of work group that is becoming increasingly important is the virtual team (or electronically mediated group) composed of people who do not necessarily meet face to face. Such groups are made possible by advances in information technology, including teleconferencing, videoconferencing, e-mail, collaborative software, and intranet-Internet systems. Globalization, plus the fact that the output of more and more teams is in the form of information or decisions rather than products or services, makes such teams ever more common. Such groups may be geographically dispersed around the world. They solve some of the problems of face-to-face multicultural groups but create others.

THE NEW-PRODUCT DEVELOPMENT TEAM

New Tech is a major producer of technology manufacturing equipment in Canada. Its employees have access to a wide range of communications technology, including videoconferencing, teleconferencing, telephone, voice mail, e-mail, and fax. The New-Product Development Team (NPD) has been formed to manage a strategic alliance with a competitor in France. The companies are co-developing products using components from each company, and they have cross-selling agreements. The team determines product specifications and is responsible for contract implementation and service. Both companies' products require extensive engineering service, which makes the team members' tasks highly interdependent. According to one team member, "A problem with a customer's equipment could arise anywhere in the world, and we might have to fix it using engineers from both companies simultaneously."

The team has eight members, three from the Canadian headquarters (including team leader Jean-Luc Dandurand), three more New Tech members from Western Europe (France, England, and Benelux), and the remaining two from the French partner. Three of the team members do not speak English fluently. The team has moderate cultural diversity. Strong differences have existed about whether members are responsible to the group or to themselves and whether careful planning or quick action is preferable.

The team met in regular two-day face-to-face meetings every two months for the first year and now meets every three months. In addition to clarifying miscommunications and making major decisions, the face-to-face meetings allow members to develop strong interpersonal relationships. Between the meetings, the members exchange information frequently (more than twice a day on average) with at least five other team members. The first preference for communication is telephone, followed by e-mail and fax. Not all members have reliable access to e-mail, and some prefer to use it only for very simple information.

So far the team has not performed up to either company's expectations, and the project is behind schedule. However, given that this is the first attempt at such a venture by either company, team members and management feel that getting this far is a major accomplishment. Product development quality is high, and customer response is good.

Jean-Luc says, "This project has had a lot of struggles. Sometimes we're behind, and they [the French partner] have the upper hand; sometimes they're behind and we have the upper hand. But we're all learning, and we're getting better, and we've had enough success in a very tough market that we intend to just keep going."[13]

The team described above is typical of global virtual teams. As shown in the case, global virtual teams need to fit their communication patterns to the task. Face-to-face communication is often interspersed with the periods of remote communication.

In virtual teams, many of the normal cues of interpersonal communication are reduced or removed, so cross-cultural differences, including language differences, are less noticeable. Yet because it may be harder to notice group processes and cultural differences, problems relating to cultural differences may be increased. Some people feel uncomfortable using electronic forms of communication, particularly for complex, novel, or subtle information. When individuals have to work with others whom they cannot see or hear directly, it is more difficult to develop trust, and groups therefore tend to develop more slowly.

These are not reasons for avoiding geographically dispersed multicultural groups—again, information technology bestows a great boon by allowing groups to interact across enormous distances. But the managers of such groups must be especially patient and must create opportunities to introduce the missing characteristics of normal group functioning to the team. Some of the keys to overcoming the difficulties of geographic dispersion (virtuality) are

- developing a shared understanding among group members about goals and group processes
- using information technology (IT) to integrate members' skills and abilities
- fitting communication patterns to the task
- developing trust among group members[14]

Making Multicultural Work Groups More Effective

Clearly the existence and extent of multicultural work groups in any organization depends on factors external to the manager: the organization's global spread and hiring policies, the composition of the available labor force, and top management support for diversity. Most managers who have to lead and supervise multicultural groups have little influence over these matters and have to accept each situation as they find it and do their best to make it productive. Many situations may be multicultural, but every situation is unique. Managing multicultural groups therefore requires not just CQ but also the knowledge and ability to perceive and take account of the group's specifics, such as

- whether the group is a team, a task force, or a crew
- whether it faces routine or complex tasks
- its degree of cultural diversity, specific cultural issues, and whether it has come to terms with these
- whether the group has a natural process for surfacing and dealing with cross-cultural issues and for ensuring that all members contribute, regardless of their cultural origins
- whether it has the characteristics required to develop its members' cultural intelligence

There may well be some culturally diverse groups that, because of the nature of their task or because they have found their own ways of functioning effectively, require little deliberate action to stimulate their cross-cultural understanding.

However, there will be other groups, particularly teams and perhaps task forces, that need to work together on complex tasks with leader/managers who are proactive in assisting them to examine, confront, and improve their processes. Cultural scripts can be so diverse and so embedded in team members that resolution requires a major effort. However, the development of cultural intelligence in the team can create a basis for mutual understanding and respect that will enable people to find their own ways to solve problems. The combination of CQ and team process skills can be a winning one.

Summary

Groups are in fashion. The popularity of team-based work environments, coupled with increasingly multicultural workforces, makes the ability to get the most from culturally diverse work teams an important current issue. In order to effectively manage or participate in multicultural work groups and teams, individuals need cultural knowledge, but also knowledge of group types, group tasks, and group structures and processes. The group itself must develop cultural intelligence, and culturally diverse groups can be an ideal place for individuals to gain greater CQ. Culturally diverse groups have the potential for both higher achievement and greater failure than single-culture groups. The trick they must perform is to maximize the positive effects of cultural diversity while minimizing its negative effects. This goal is achievable by high-CQ leaders who also use group-process knowledge, practice mindfulness in group interactions, adapt behavior to accommodate the unique circumstances of the group, and encourage and train members to become culturally intelligent.

CHAPTER 8

Developing Cultural Intelligence in an Interconnected World

Barbara Bull, the American public relations officer of a Beijing hotel, was annoyed with Weixing Li, a Chinese staff member who had repeatedly turned up late.

"Do you know what you did wrong?"

His response was a blank stare.

"Do you know what you did wrong? Do you know why I am upset?"

Another blank look.

"Do you know what you did wrong?"

"Whatever you say I did wrong, I did wrong," he replied.

Barbara was taken aback. What did he mean? "I want you to tell me what you did wrong!" she said.

"Whatever you say I did wrong, I did wrong. You are the boss. Whatever you say is correct. So whatever you say I did wrong, I admit to."

This made her even angrier. So she told him exactly what he had done wrong, describing his irresponsibility, immaturity, and failure. He apologized and said no more. He looked downcast. Did he understand the problem? Would he change?

Later, Barbara had a conversation with her fellow manager

Chrissie, who has been in China for several years. When Barbara described what had happened, Chrissie nodded. What Barbara had experienced, she explained, was a common problem. Barbara simply did not understand the importance of *mianzi* to Chinese people.

"*Mianzi* is what Westerners would call 'face,' as in 'saving face' or 'losing face.' In Chinese culture it is the motivating force behind many actions. Chinese employees tend to see things from a hierarchical viewpoint. Weixing probably knew he had done something wrong, but he would have handled it by letting his boss point out what he should have done. Instead, you made him lose face, which was bad for his commitment to the company, though fortunately you didn't reprimand him in front of others. But he would see the loss of face as applying not just to himself but to you. Instead, you might have explained how his actions had caused both you and the company to lose face. That would have caused him shame, and he might have learned."

"Wow! I'll try to remember that next time I want to blow my top. But being in a foreign country is like walking on eggshells. People's egos are so easily crushed. How am I supposed to know these things? How can I practice?"

This case presents a paradox of cultural intelligence. The paradox is this:

> In order to acquire cultural intelligence you must practice, by living and working in culturally different environments, or by working with culturally different people.

But

> In order to live and work effectively in culturally different environments, or to work successfully with culturally different people, you first need to acquire cultural intelligence.

This is a difficult problem. It means that Barbara and Weixing and others like them must do two things at once: continuously observe and learn cultural intelligence at the same time as they practice it. Barbara was too intent on getting Weixing to diagnose his own error, and Weixing held on to his Chinese beliefs about hierarchical relationships. Perhaps both will learn enough from their encounter for it to transfer to the next intercultural situation. And by sharing the problem with an experienced colleague, Barbara has been able to add to the knowledge component of her cultural intelligence. This aspect of the case reminds us that cultural intelligence is not developed through mere exposure to other cultures but requires conscious effort.

Characteristics Supportive of Cultural Intelligence

Some characteristics that individuals already possess or can develop make them more willing and better able to increase their cultural intelligence. For example, personality traits such as openness to new experience, extroversion, and agreeableness, improve the capacity to acquire the necessary skills. Again, mindfulness is key because, combined with the active pursuit of opportunities for cross-cultural interaction, it lays a foundation for developing greater cultural intelligence.

Developmental Stages of CQ

The development of cultural intelligence occurs in several stages.

> *Stage 1: Reactivity* to external stimuli. The starting point is a mindless adherence to one's own cultural norms, typical of people with little exposure to, or interest in, other cultures. These people may not even recognize that cultural differences exist, or may consider them inconsequential. They may say things like "I don't see differences. I treat everyone the same."
>
> *Stage 2: Recognition* of other cultural norms and motivation to learn more about them. Experience and mindfulness produce a new awareness of the multicultural mosaic

around us. The individual is curious and wants to learn more but may struggle with the complexity of the cultural environment and search for simple rules to guide behavior.

Stage 3: Accommodation of other cultural norms in one's own mind. Reliance on absolutes disappears. A deeper understanding of cultural variation begins to develop. Different cultural norms and rules become comprehensible and even reasonable in their context. The individual knows what to say and do in different cultural situations but finds it difficult to adapt and often feels awkward.

Stage 4: Assimilation of diverse cultural norms into alternative behaviors. At this stage, adjusting to different situations no longer requires much effort. Individuals develop a repertoire of behaviors from which they can choose depending on the situation. They function in different cultures effortlessly, almost as if they were in their home cultures. Members of other cultures accept them and feel comfortable interacting with them. They feel at home almost anywhere.

Stage 5: Proactivity in cultural behavior based on recognition of changes in cues that others do not notice and changes in cultural context, sometimes even before members of the other culture recognize them. Individuals at this stage are so attuned to the nuances of intercultural interactions that they automatically adjust their behavior in anticipation and know how to execute it effectively. Such individuals may be rare, but they demonstrate a level of cultural intelligence to which we might all aspire.

Culturally intelligent people have a *cognitively complex* perception of their environment. They can make connections between seemingly disparate pieces of information. They describe people and events in terms of many different characteristics and can see the many links among these characteristics and the coherent pattern in a cultural situation. They see past the stereotypes that a superficial understanding of cultural dimensions—such as collectivism, uncertainty avoidance, and power distance (Chapter 2)—provides. Knowledge of these dimensions is only a first step in developing cultural intelligence.[1] Culturally intelligent people see the connections between a culture and its context, history, and values.

The Process of Developing Cultural Intelligence

Raising your CQ requires experience-based learning that can take considerable time. You need a base level of knowledge, the acquisition of new knowledge and alternative perspectives through mindfulness, and the development of this knowledge into behavioral skills. The process is iterative and can be thought of as a series of S curves, as shown in Figure 8.1.[2]

The acquisition of cultural intelligence involves learning from social interactions. Such social learning is a very powerful way of transferring experiences into knowledge and skills.[3] Social learning involves *attention* to the situation, *retention* of the knowledge gained from the situation, *reproduction* of the behavioral skills observed, and finally *reinforcement* (receiving feedback) about the effectiveness of the adapted behavior.

Improving CQ by learning from social experience means paying attention to, and appreciating, critical cultural differences between oneself and others. This requires knowledge about how cultures differ and how culture affects behavior, awareness of contextual cues, and openness to the legitimacy and importance of different behavior. To retain this knowledge, we must transfer our learning from the specific experience to later interactions in other settings. To reproduce the skills, we need to practice them in future interactions. To reinforce the skills, we need to try out behaviors frequently and mindfully.

As implied by Figure 8.1, improving your CQ takes time, and you must be motivated to do it. The iterative and long-

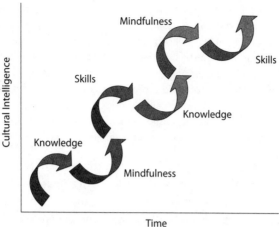

FIGURE 8.1. The development of cultural intelligence

term nature of gaining cultural intelligence is illustrated in the following example.

UNDERSTANDING THE FRENCH

Jenny Stephens, a U.S. national, is an executive for the French subsidiary of an American multinational. After meeting and marrying a Frenchman in New York, she moved to Paris, where she has lived for seven years. She speaks French fluently and regularly interacts with French relatives and friends and colleagues. When asked if she feels she understands French culture, she says

> I have been here for seven years. I have found that whenever I would begin to get a sense that I really understand the French, something strange would happen that would throw me off completely. As I would reflect on the event and discuss it with my husband and friends, I would develop a more complex view of the French. Then, things would go fine for several months until the whole process would repeat itself.
>
> For example, I felt I was making progress when I learned how to buy cheese. Putting together a proper cheese plate in France is as complicated as choosing wine correctly. A perfect

> cheese presentation must contain five cheeses—a ripe (but not too ripe) light, soft cheese; a hard, sharp cheese; a goat cheese; a semisoft cheese; and a blue cheese. However, just knowing this is insufficient to be viewed as anything but a novice in a French cheese shop. To be truly expert, one must know what cheeses from what regions are particularly good at the moment. When I learned that by simply using my basic knowledge and asking appropriate questions such as what brie is particularly good this week, I was treated with much more respect.[4]

In this case Jenny is practicing mindfulness by recognizing unusual things that she observes as being related to culture and talking them over with others. She also uses mindfulness when she recognizes that her limited knowledge can be used effectively by planning how to adapt her behavior. In this way, each instance of idiosyncratic French behavior builds on her previous knowledge and contributes to her development of cultural intelligence.

Activities That Support the Development of Cultural Intelligence

Perhaps the most important means of increasing cultural intelligence is spending time in foreign countries, in which cross-cultural experiences will be frequent and CQ will increase through necessity. While foreign experiences are ideal, there are numerous other situations and activities you can draw upon, ranging from formal education to informal interactions, including developing relationships with others who are culturally different.

FORMAL EDUCATION/TRAINING

The types of formal training available on cultural intelligence can be classified in terms of being experience-based (as opposed to purely "classroom") and being culture-specific or applicable across cultures. All these types are valuable, but cultural intelligence requires learning from experience and building skills that can be applied *across* cultures. The following chart shows the types of formal training available and how they apply to our model of developing a high CQ.

TRAINING TYPE	TRAINING METHOD	APPLICATION TO CQ
Factual	Books, lectures, films, area briefings	Knowledge about specific cultures, culture dimensions, and processes
Analytical	Case study analysis, discussion, culture assimilators (self-administered, programmed culture-training manuals)	Both culture-general and culture-specific knowledge as well as the opportunity to practice mindfulness
Experiential	Simulations, role-playing, field trips, actual intercultural experience (at home or abroad)	Opportunities to practice both mindfulness and behavior skills, and to experience the emotions of cross-cultural interaction

Of the three types of methods, formal experiential training is the most rigorous and effective but is rare and often expensive. Most of us therefore rely on our day-to-day interactions with culturally different others, in different contexts: multicultural teams, interactions with culturally different individuals at home, and foreign assignments.

MULTICULTURAL GROUPS AND TEAMS

Because of globalization, our work groups are increasingly multicultural, offering rich opportunities to gain cultural intelligence by observing the behavior of individuals from different cultures responding to the same situations. Examples include the assignment of group roles, the establishment of a leader, and the imposition of deadlines. If we are mindful, we will note the wide variety of reactions from culturally different members to the group's behavior. The interactions of culturally different people in groups are complex, but this complexity generates great learning opportunities to develop greater cultural intelligence.

The numerous learning opportunities that multicultural societies present us with often lack the depth and intensity that is required for us to learn from them. For a Westerner, having dinner at a Cantonese restaurant and interacting with the Chinese service people is indeed an intercultural experience, but it is a very mild one (although it might become a bit more intense with an order of chicken feet!) and lacks significant engagement. Just as leadership skills are often taught by testing the leaders of groups engaged in challenging outdoor activities such as ropes courses, significant CQ development requires us to move outside our comfort zone and to challenge ourselves in deeper ways.

In our international management courses we, the authors, routinely require our students to practice the skills they have learned in class by engaging in a non-trivial cross-cultural experience in their local area. "Culture" in this case is not confined to national or ethnic culture but, consistent with our definition in Chapter 2, can be applied to any social group. Subcultures within a culture provide excellent learning experiences. We tell students that if they are to learn, they should feel culturally uncomfortable in the situation, at least at first. Some ways to engage in cross-cultural experiences are to

- Locate an ethnic organization in your community and attend (and participate in, if possible) a cultural celebration. Ask members to explain the significance of the event and the symbolism of the activities.
- Find an interest group that represents a set of beliefs to which you do not subscribe and attend one of its meetings. For example, some of our heterosexual university

students have attended meetings of gay and lesbian associations.

- Attend a religious service or wedding ceremony of someone from another culture. Ask a member of the culture to explain the significance of the rituals involved. One of our mature MBA students, a Japanese-Canadian, visited the home and attended the temple of a Sikh co-worker. The following is an excerpt from her report.[5]

MY CROSS-CULTURAL DAY WITH ANANYA

For my cross-cultural experience I was fortunate to spend the day with Ananya, who is an IT specialist at my organization. I was invited to her home and to accompany her to the Sikh *Gurdwara* (temple) in East Vancouver. I wanted to embrace this opportunity not only for the experience but also because I looked forward to getting to know her. The objective of the experience was to practice mindfulness in order to increase my cultural intelligence and be more effective in a variety of cross-cultural situations. Over the weeks following my visit with Ananya, I re-examined some of my past and present experiences as well as my thoughts and opinions. I realized that despite being different, I had become desensitized and had oversimplified the influence of culture around me. I had always believed that I instinctively knew more than others because of my history of being simultaneously Canadian and Japanese but never fitting into either world. However I realized that just because I am bicultural, it does not make me an expert in operating cross-culturally.

In preparation for my day with Ananya I read to gain some basic knowledge about her culture. It was helpful to read about Indian facts and culture on the Country Insights page of the Government of Canada website and the information on the Internet about Sikhism. This information allowed me to learn appropriate behavior at the temple and to develop expectations about her home.

Some aspects of Ananya's home were a surprise, such as how her children, who were born in Canada, respected and lived the family value system in a deep way. The family had custom-designed their current home to a duplex and laneway house so that the parents and their two adult children are able to live multi-generationally together. This is a cultural norm. We drank the chai tea that she prepared for us and talked. I learned about how she practices her beliefs through the twice-daily prayer and washing. This helps her overcome the frustrations of a bad work day. The scriptures teach to remove negative thoughts before going to bed.

At the temple my head was appropriately covered. I followed her to the women's side of the entrance hall where we removed our shoes and washed our hands. We walked into the main hall, and I bowed when she bowed. We then accepted the Karah-parshad pudding. I became overwhelmed in the moment and did not cup both hands. I was embarrassed, but the woman dishing out the pudding gave me the slightest of smiles and demonstrated without speaking. Could this have been a smile of disapproval? I was not sure. I immediately corrected my behavior. We found a place to sit with the women, and I listened to the singing of the Gurbani while I read the English translation upon the large screen. It spoke of human frailty, and the beautiful music was both enchanting and sad.

We left upon Ananya's signal and joined in the sharing of a meal in the Langar halls at communal tables. Did I feel uncomfortable that day? I know I attracted some attention, but (as a Japanese-Canadian) my normal is to be different in a crowd. Consistent with Sikh beliefs, I felt welcome to be there. Being immersed in this situation and operating with heightened awareness was a good reminder of what it feels like to be different. I realized that over time I had dialed down my sensitivity and have been on "cultural cruise control." During my day with Ananya, I did work hard to observe, and it took constant attention. However I found that questioning why did not come automatically. Too many times I subconsciously answered my own questions with assumptions, which typically were based upon stereotypes. These were lost opportunities to gain a deeper understanding. When I returned home I did some more reading and was better able to appreciate my experience in the *Gurdwara*. I found that my retention for cultural details improved, this second time being able to put the knowledge into an experiential context. Continuous learning is important to increasing cultural intelligence.

A key takeaway from my experience is to be more mindful of the needs of my co-workers when we converse about an issue. Often if a person was frustrated at work, I had, over time, developed a script. I listened to identify the problem and honed in on the impact to the individual whom I assumed was looking for a resolution. This is the approach that is common in individualistic cultures. However on my day with Ananya, I learned I need to be mindful that some people have great concern or greater concern about the group than others. In order to satisfy their need for resolution, I must remember to address issues at multiple levels, particularly for those with a collectivist orientation.

This bicultural student's experience with her colleague is a good example of mindfulness in action and the development of cultural intelligence. Her immersion into a culturally different situation showed her how often she had operated on cultural cruise control, and her description of the situation shows acute attention to the behavior of those who are culturally different from her, as well as to the context. As this case shows, you can find cross-cultural interactions in your own backyard as well as abroad. These learning experiences can translate very directly to participants' daily lives at home or in the workplace.

FOREIGN EXPERIENCE AND EXPATRIATE ASSIGNMENTS

One of the most challenging ways of confronting cultural differences is living and working in a foreign country for a temporary period.

BUT I AM CHINESE!

Changying, a Chinese American with a master's degree in international business who is fluent in Chinese, had taken an assignment in China with a multinational firm. She felt she would be a bridge between the firm's Chinese and American managers, but she was surprised to find that she had misunderstood the environment. After a year she noted: "My understanding of managing effectively came primarily from trial and error. I learned the hard way, falling on my face. But each time I fell, I'd assess what the critical learning of each incident was. When accepting an overseas assignment one must have an open mind. China has one of the highest expatriate assignment failure rates in the world, and inability to manage across cultures is the most important reason, because expatriates fail to understand the thought processes and motivation of local employees."[6]

As this case demonstrates, cultural intelligence is often gained by trying out new behaviors and observing their effect, even when they don't work out as planned. Also, the observation that understanding how local employees think is important to expatriate success cannot be overemphasized. Foreign visits and assignments require, perhaps more than any other situation, that you try to understand the behavior of others in terms of their own cultural background. They offer opportunities for intense experiential learning. If, like most people, you have had very little cross-cultural training before going overseas, you will have to adjust on the fly.

In foreign experience, unlike work in multicultural teams, we are typically focused on the single culture in which we are immersed, and the experience consequently tends to be intense and emotionally charged, causing high stress levels until we adjust. When everything seems to be working against us, it is difficult to see the situation as a meaningful learning experience.

Figure 8.2 shows a model of the phases that some experts believe people go through as they adjust to a foreign environment.[7] The process follows a U-shaped curve through a honeymoon period, culture shock, attempted adjustment, and then mastery. In the honeymoon stage everything is new and exciting, as it would be to a short-term tourist. In fact,

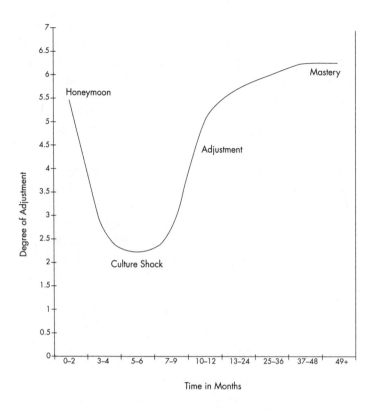

FIGURE 8.2.   The U-curve of cross-cultural adjustment

most fast-moving tourists never get beyond this stage, making tourism often too shallow an experience for the development of cultural intelligence. In the culture-shock stage, the differences between what the expatriate is used to and what the new culture provides become apparent, as the individual either learns—including developing his or her CQ—or fails to learn, how to adapt. Those with high CQ get into the routines and rhythms of daily life in the new country and move eventually to mastery, while others never properly adjust.

A real possibility for some people is that the adjustment is so successful and their view of the new country so positive that they lose all desire to return home. Others meet romantic partners in the new environment, and the couple must make the tough decision about which of them will make the other's country home.

BREAKUP IN BEIJING

For Dublin natives Jonathan and Julie Henderson, Jonathan's move from his corporate position in Amsterdam to Regional Vice President for Asia seemed like a wonderful opportunity: a big promotion and salary raise, the chance for the couple and their children to experience Asian culture, a home in a luxurious expatriate development with good schools for their two children, a minimum three-year contract with a guaranteed subsequent job in South America, and a part-time job for Julie in Beijing with the HR consultancy she had worked for in Europe. It was a chance the adventurous Hendersons were up for. They traveled to China with high hopes.

But two years later it seemed that everything that could go wrong had gone wrong. First of all there were minor problems: the move had not been handled well by HR at Jonathan's company, there were unexpected expenses due to Chinese bureaucracy, and communication was either too indirect or was hampered by poor English skills among some of the locals in Jonathan's organization. Then there were contextual discomforts: high air pollution, poor sanitation, difficulties in sourcing food secure from contamination, living in a compound cut off from proper cultural experience and having the children gawked at by locals whenever they went out. In addition, Jonathan's job required much more travel than he had expected. Julie, left at home with an *ayi* (maid) to look after the family, felt under increasing stress. This was compounded when their two sons each suffered major medical problems and she realized the frightening inadequacy of local medical resources. She even had to travel with one child to Hong Kong to ensure adequate treatment. And the children said they didn't like China; they couldn't relate to the locals, and they missed their Irish relations, who they had seen a lot when they were in Amsterdam. Their unhappiness upset Julie further. When did I sign up for this? she thought.

Two years into the assignment, Julie went to her hometown, Dublin, for a work-related conference, where she also met up with her Irish family. In Dublin, the children enjoyed a happy reunion with their grandparents and other relations, and Julie was unexpectedly offered the job of her dreams, with a global consulting firm. And in her own home town! Time for the family to repatriate, surely? But Jonathan was contractually obligated to continue in his job in Beijing for another year and did not want to break his link with the company and perhaps jeopardize his entire career. Reluctantly, the family agreed to split up for at least the next year, Jonathan remaining in Beijing while Julie re-settled in Dublin with the children.[8]

This case shows that cross-cultural issues may be only one of many factors affecting expatriate assignments that may cause problems for assignees, their organizations, and their families. As a result, many organizations operating internationally are re-thinking their whole approach to such assignments, with alternatives including shorter stays, flying visits, and more employment of locals. On the other hand, some expatriates find living overseas a very positive, sometimes life-changing experience.

As the case also shows, cultural intelligence may be important for the whole family. If you want your children to grow up with a high CQ in a world that will increasingly value it, why not give them a taste of international experience while they are still young and flexible enough to make the most of it? They will need support and guidance, but gaining cultural intelligence as a family will be a great experience.

For those in international organizations, employers can assist adjustment to overseas postings by providing appropriate training. There is evidence that cross-cultural training assists with overseas adjustment, relationships with host nationals, and employee performance. However, some organizations believe cross-cultural training is not effective and do not provide it. If you have been given this book by your company as part of an education program, it is a sign that the company is giving some thought to these important issues. If your staff has cross-cultural issues, consider giving copies to them.

Margaret is English. She has always enjoyed travel. At nineteen, she traveled for two years in Europe. She funded her travel mainly by working in Greece as a bartender and even gained supervisory experience in a restaurant. Her European experience sparked an interest in both history and in business. So on her return to the UK, she went to university to study history and economics.

When she finished the degree, Margaret decided on a career in teaching. But she first wanted to travel again, so she gained a place with JET (Japanese Exchange Teaching)—teaching English to adults in Japan, an opportunity she thought would be culturally, linguistically, educationally, and financially valuable to her. Her assignment carried a two-year contract.

Margaret settled well into the JET work in Osaka, where she was soon approached by a local government organization wanting to hire her to set up an English-language program for its employees— an opportunity for further personal and professional development. Her students were well motivated, and this six months of additional part-time work helped Margaret to add to her savings and gave her a friendly social circle. She took trips around Japan with her adult student friends.

Margaret also had enough money and time away from teaching to do about three months' touring per year in Asia. She traveled with an American friend, a colleague in the JET program. Meantime Mama-san and Papa-san—a café-owner couple with whom she boarded, adopted her almost as if she were their own daughter. They showed her around, taught her about Japanese ways, communicated with her only in Japanese, and gave her part-time work in the café. Margaret's cultural learning was dramatic.

After two years, Margaret became aware that she wanted to return to Britain. She wanted to see her parents and brothers again, and she wanted to own her own home. As to her teaching career, she thought about the rudeness and poor self-discipline of British school students and compared them unfavorably to those of her polite and motivated adult Japanese students. She realized how poorly paid teachers were. She returned to the UK with some money but no real plan. She bought a small house in her home city.

She got a job as a sales rep for a company selling database solutions and soon realized that she had found her forte—selling. Then, two years ago, she was approached by a software company and took a sales job with it. The job is good but doesn't utilize all her energy or fulfill all her interests. She aspires to start her own business. She learned a lot from Mama-san and Papa-san and the way they had turned their little Osaka café into a gold mine! But she feels she lacks skills and knowledge relating to the wider business world, so she has enrolled for an MBA. She has a business plan—to start an export-based Internet company selling British products overseas. She sees Japan as a key market and believes her understanding of the language and culture will assist her greatly.

Among the things Margaret learned overseas were the Japanese language (and a smattering of other Asian languages), patience, and what she calls "cultural sensitivity"—particularly how to interact with Asians, an ability she uses a lot with Indian and Chinese staff in her current employment. Overseas, she gained self-knowledge, self-confidence, and a broader perspective. She enhanced her cooking skills, her ability to speak in public, even her abilities in her sport, judo. And of course she now has a special interest in, and affinity for, Asia, especially Japan and its people, and good contacts there. She knows Japan will continue to be important in her life.[9]

Margaret's self-initiated expatriation has not only dramatically increased her cultural intelligence, it has transformed her entire life, including her employment, her long-term ambitions, and her identity. She is now much more of a citizen of the world. In her determined internationalism, she is typical of many of today's young people. They want to see the world. Because employment in other cultures forces us to come to grips with those cultures, young people increasingly work as they travel, and the acquisition of cultural intelligence is integrated with their career development. As one returnee from extended foreign travel put it

> I have learned to look at the world around me with a childlike wonder and to drop any preconceived notions.... I have learned that just because I have grown up indoctrinated by a certain set of rules regarding how relationships and society in general work, that does not make them universally true or right.

If you are a middle-aged reader and are thinking, "Gee, I wish I had thought like that when I was young," it's never too late. Talk to your children about it!

ACQUIRING CQ THROUGH OVERSEAS EXPERIENCE

As shown previously, spending time living and working abroad is an important way of developing cultural intelligence. But it does not happen automatically. It requires a significant inter-action with the new culture, providing the opportunity to practice mindfulness and develop cross-cultural skills. Some leading companies use global experiential programs in which high-potential employees work in multicultural groups to solve problems in developing countries. An example is Project Ulysses at PricewaterhouseCoopers.[10]

PROJECT ULYSSES

PricewaterhouseCoopers (PwC) consists of legally independent firms in 150 countries and employs more than 160,000 people (5 percent of whom are partners). Project Ulysses is an integrated service-learning program initiated by PwC in 2001. Participants are sent in multicultural teams of three or four to developing countries to work with NGOs, social entrepreneurs, or international organizations. These teams work on a pro bono basis in eight-week field assignments helping communities deal with the effects of poverty, conflict, and environmental degradation. As of 2008,

120 PwC partners from thirty-five different countries participated in the program. The overall goal of the project was to develop global leaders in PwC's worldwide network of firms. In reporting on the leadership needs of PwC, Ralf Schneider, a PwC partner based in Frankfurt and head of global talent development said, "It was clear it was not going to be a standard business model with a standard leader. We needed to take people outside of that box." Knowledge gained by individuals is transferred back to the organization not only by participants resuming their jobs but also through formal debriefing sessions that permit PwC to continuously refine the Ulysses model.

Examples of the project teams are the following:

Brian McCann, a PwC client service partner from Boston who specializes in mergers and acquisitions was the only U.S. member of the 2003 Belize team that included colleagues from Malaysia, Sweden, and Germany. Their mission was to work with Ya'axché Conservation Trust to evaluate the growth and income-generating potential of the eco-tourism market in southern Belize where 50 percent of the population is unemployed and 75 percent earn less than U.S.$200 a month. Brian reported that the learning experience from both a personal and a professional perspective was profound.

Dinu Bumbacea, a PwC partner from Romania, and his teammates from Thailand, Australia, and the UK worked with the Elias Mutale Training Centre in Kasama, Zambia, along with the United Nations Development Program and Africare on a strategy for economic diversification in the region. Dinu said that the experience gave him new insight into operating in a multicultural environment and team, and in dealing with the public sector.

Programs such as Project Ulysses provide cultural intelligence development opportunities combined from both multicultural teams and overseas experience. However, not everyone is fortunate enough to work for organizations with such extensive programs.

You can of course develop cultural intelligence from overseas experience without such formal programs. However, you will need to prepare, focus, and be mindful. Every cross-cultural incident—at your work, in social life, even when shopping—will be an opportunity to reflect, to learn, and to experiment. You will need to be in the right *frame of mind* to acquire CQ. Why are you going overseas? What do you want from the experience? Escaping a bad situation at home or hoping for career advancement on return may not be the best motivation. Self-development, a desire for adventure, a wish to broaden your horizons and meet new kinds of people, or a sense of mission are better. They will help you to live in the here and now and to take a genuine interest in your new environment and its people.

You will need to *prepare*. Read all you can about the new country you are to visit and find out about its cultural background. Study the cultural dimensions we introduced in Chapter 2, and try to figure out where your new home fits in. Seek out people who have been there, and ask them about their experiences. Consider also the various personal issues involved (such as those experienced by the Hendersons in the earlier case), including potential effects on compensation, family life, social networks, lifestyle, health, career, and stress.[11]

In many foreign locations there are opportunities for new-comers to feel at home—restaurants and communities set up by expatriates, international hotels modeled on Western norms and standards, and even, for example in Saudi Arabia and China, compounds or housing developments designed for specific groups of foreigners. To develop cultural intelligence, you should avoid the temptation of spending all your time in these environments, which are essentially just extensions of home. Remember our advice to get out of your comfort zone, and seek genuinely local experiences.

As in the cases of the Hendersons and Margaret, the most common reason that people return early from overseas is family issues. Make sure your relationships with family members you are leaving behind are considered. Involve family members who are going overseas with you in the preparation, and support them in the adventure. It is their opportunity to acquire cultural intelligence too, and their adjustment is just as important as your own.

You will have to be self-forgiving and patient. Even with plenty of preparation, you will doubtless make mistakes. Your performance in the first year abroad is unlikely to be your best. You may sometimes need to laugh at your own inadequacies and to remember that you can learn from even negative experiences.

The future for many is not just intercultural but international. We, and our children and grandchildren, will more and more have to be able to feel at home wherever we are and to function with the ease and familiarity that is habitual to us at home. The opportunity to travel to foreign countries is precious. The investment is our time and aspirations and the energy we give to the process. Part of the dividend we receive is enhanced cultural intelligence. As we hope this book has shown, the reward will be well worth the effort.

Rules of Cross-Cultural Engagement

Last, regardless of the specific cultural context, there are several rules of engagement for interactions with others who are culturally different. Become knowledgeable about your own culture and background, its biases and idiosyncrasies, and how these are unconsciously reflected in your own perceptions and actions.

- Deliberately avoid mindlessness: expect differences in others. See different behavior as novel, and suspend evaluation of it.

- Switch into a mindful mode, becoming attentive to behavioral cues, what they may mean, and the likely effect of your behavior on others.

- Adapt your behavior in ways that you are comfortable with and believe are appropriate for the situation.
- Be mindful of responses to your behavioral adaptation.
- Experiment with adapting intuitively to new situations, and use these experiments to help you acquire a repertoire of new behaviors.
- Practice new behaviors that work until they become automatic.

Summary

Developing cultural intelligence requires experiences that involve both acquiring knowledge and applying mindfulness. Such development involves a series of stages, from simply reacting to external stimuli to proactively adjusting behavior in anticipation of changes in the cultural context. Some underlying individual characteristics support this development. Ways of developing cultural intelligence can include formal education and training, but experiential learning, for which our multicultural environment provides many opportunities, is critical. Time spent living and working overseas is an excellent way to improve cultural intelligence, but one should first know a good deal about oneself, and one should understand the phenomenon of culture shock and the process of adjustment. Practicing mindfulness enhances this ability. Following a few simple guidelines for intercultural interactions can assist in developing the ability to act competently across cultures, adding a valuable skill to your repertoire.

The Essentials
of Cultural Intelligence

The twenty-first-century world is increasingly global, and relating effectively to others who are culturally different has become a daily necessity. This globalization is being fueled by dramatic economic shifts in many countries and by advances in communications technology. We may not travel the world, but the world has come to us. We have to deal daily with international issues and transactions, and with people from other countries and cultures.

Despite rapid modernization, culture is slow to change. For the foreseeable future, cultural differences will remain a key factor in interpersonal interactions. And we have long known that in the organizations where we spend most of our time—both those we work in and those we are customers of—interacting effectively with others is the most important part of our lives. In an increasingly competitive world, individuals who do not keep their skills up to date run the risk of losing out. Organizations that do not develop these skills in their employees risk falling behind their competitors.

In this book, we have introduced what we believe to be a key competency for the twenty-first century: *cultural intelligence*. Cultural intelligence, the capability to deal effectively

159

with people from different cultural backgrounds, is a multifaceted competency consisting of cultural *knowledge,* the practice of *mindfulness,* and a repertoire of *cross-cultural skills.*

In order to get a sense of your current level of cultural intelligence, go to the back of the book and complete the short form of the Cultural Intelligence Assessment in the appendix. The higher you score on this assessment, the higher your level of cultural intelligence is likely to be.

As shown in Chapter 8 (Figure 8.1), cultural intelligence is developed through repetitive experiences over time, in which each repetition of the cycle builds on the previous one. The feedback from each cycle of experience leads to an ever-higher cultural intelligence quotient, or CQ. In this way, specific knowledge gained in both formal and informal ways is transformed into an ability that can then be applied to new situations.

Culture has a profound influence on almost all aspects of human endeavor. The culturally intelligent person has special *knowledge.* He or she understands the possible effects of cultural variation (e.g., differences in values) on his or her own behavior and that of others. The culturally intelligent person also knows how and in what circumstances these cultural differences are likely to have an effect. Culture matters, but it doesn't matter to the same degree in all circumstances all the time.

Cultural intelligence also requires the practice of mindfulness. Mindfulness is

- being aware of our own assumptions, ideas, and emotions
- noticing what is apparent about the other person's assumptions, words, and behavior
- using all of the senses in perceiving situations
- viewing the situation from several perspectives
- attending to the context to help interpret what is happening

- creating new mental maps of others
- creating new and more sophisticated categories for others
- seeking out fresh information to confirm or disconfirm mental maps
- using empathy

Knowledge and mindfulness are key elements of cultural intelligence, but in themselves they are not enough. Becoming culturally intelligent means acquiring cross-cultural *skills*. It is not just about becoming more skilled but also about developing a repertoire of skilled behaviors and knowing when to use each one. While everyone can learn to be culturally intelligent, certain characteristics of individuals, such as openness, extraversion, and agreeableness, support the development of cultural intelligence.

- Culturally intelligent *decision makers* understand the different ways in which people with different cultural backgrounds mentally simplify the complex decision-making process. They know their own motivation and goals in making decisions, and they understand how the motivations, goals, and decision-making methods of people from other cultures might differ from their own. They also know that cultural factors may sometimes outweigh Western concepts of rationality. They are mindful of the ethical components of business decisions and the relationship of ethical behavior to their underlying cultural values. Finally, they are able to adapt decision-making behavior, such as the type and amount of information gathered, the weighting of decision criteria, and the degree of participation in decisions that is appropriate to the specific cultural context, while at the same time respecting the universal rights of all those involved.

- Culturally intelligent *communicators* and *negotiators* know that cultural differences have a huge influence on the communication and negotiation processes. In organizations we spend most of our time in communication with others, and in no other activity is people's cultural grounding more influential. Both language and nonverbal behavior make it tricky to communicate across cultures. Culturally intelligent negotiators know how to anticipate communication differences, practice mindfulness by paying attention to both the context and the conventions of communication as well as its content, and adapt their negotiation behavior to make concessions, persuade, exchange information, and/or build relationships as appropriate for the negotiation and the cultural context.

- Culturally intelligent *leaders* know that leadership exists largely in the minds of followers. While all followers expect leaders to have a vision, to be able to communicate that vision, and to have skill in organizing followers, the specific behaviors that they use to do these things vary dramatically across cultures. The culturally intelligent leader understands that his or her leadership style will be largely either task- or relationship-oriented but that some adaptation of this style may be required depending on the characteristics of followers (e.g., their degree of collectivism). Culturally intelligent leaders do not unthinkingly mimic the leadership behaviors of another culture. Rather, they pay close attention to leaders like themselves who are effective in the cross-cultural environment and model their behavior appropriately.

- Culturally intelligent *team members* and *leaders* know that culturally diverse work groups and teams have the potential for very high achievement but also characteristics that make them prone to failure. The key to managing culturally diverse work groups lies in maximizing the benefits of diversity while minimizing the costs. Culturally intelligent team management also requires fostering cultural intelligence among team members. In order to do this, team members and team leaders must understand the effects of group processes and the steps to cultural intelligence. Team managers must consider the effects of group type, the nature of the group task, the cultural diversity of the group, and the group's internal processes to resolve conflict.

The development of cultural intelligence is an iterative process. Each intercultural interaction in which we engage offers the opportunity to enhance our cultural intelligence. Cultural intelligence can be developed at home. However, for a person seeking cultural intelligence, a period of time living and working overseas, either self-initiated or as a company assignment or training program, can be extremely rewarding.

We wish that we could somehow endow you with high cultural intelligence or that you could download it from the Internet. But developing cultural intelligence will involve hard work on your part. It is essentially a process based in *experience*. As such, it is often both physically and emotionally taxing. However, we think the sense of confidence and control in cross-cultural interactions that you will feel will make it worth the effort. We hope this book has helped you to start on this journey.

Appendix:
Short Form Cultural Intelligence Assessment

This measure is the result of ten years of academic research on cultural intelligence funded by Social Sciences and Humanities Research Council of Canada. It was developed in response to the need for an easy-to-administer assessment of individual differences in cultural intelligence. The research project that led to its development was headed by the first author of this book and involved dozens of university researchers around the world.

SFCQ

Below are ten statements about one's experience when interacting with people from other cultures. Please indicate to what extent each of the following statements describes you.

	NOT AT ALL	A LITTLE	SOME-WHAT	A LOT	EXTREMELY WELL
1. I know the ways in which cultures around the world are different.	1	2	3	4	5
2. I can give examples of cultural differences from my personal experience, reading, and so on.	1	2	3	4	5
3. I enjoy talking with people from different cultures.	1	2	3	4	5
4. I have the ability to accurately understand the feelings of people from other cultures.	1	2	3	4	5
5. I sometimes try to understand people from another culture by imagining how something looks from their perspective.	1	2	3	4	5
6. I can change my behavior to suit different cultural situations and people.	1	2	3	4	5
7. I accept delays without becoming upset when in different cultural situations and with culturally different people.	1	2	3	4	5

	NOT AT ALL	A LITTLE	SOME- WHAT	A LOT	EXTREMELY WELL
8. I am aware of the cultural knowledge I use when interacting with someone from another culture.	1	2	3	4	5
9. I think a lot about the influence that culture has on my behavior and that of others who are culturally different.	1	2	3	4	5
10. I am aware that I need to plan my course of action when in different cultural situations and with culturally different people.	1	2	3	4	5

USING THE SFCQ

Your score is the average value for the ten items.

In a sample of more than 3500 individuals from around the world, the average score was 3.51 with a standard deviation of .63.

If you answer the questions honestly, the SFCQ is a good indicator of your present level of CQ.

IMPORTANT FINDINGS REGARDING THE SFCQ

The SFCQ scale has been shown to be equivalent across cultures and has been administered in English, French,

Indonesian, Turkish, and traditional Chinese. We know it measures CQ effectively in different languages and cultures.

The SFCQ is related to, but distinct from, emotional intelligence and personality. While some individual characteristics might lead to the development of CQ, we know that it is a unique element of an individual's makeup.

The SFCQ is positively related to the number of languages individuals speak and their international experience (the number of countries they have lived in and the number of countries they have visited), and it is negatively related to their degree of ethnocentrism. This confirms that CQ is developed through experience.

The SFCQ predicts overall effectiveness in cross-cultural situations and job performance in a culturally diverse environment. It also predicts an individual's ability to develop long-term relationships with culturally different people (e.g., if s/he has a good friend or a best friend from another culture). The SFCQ also predicts the ability of individuals to correctly assess the causes of behavior displayed by those of different cultures. In summary and as expected, CQ indicates the ability that individuals have to be effective in dealing with those from a different culture and in culturally challenging situations.

Because the SFCQ is a self-report measure, individuals can give answers that they think are desirable instead of being honest with themselves about their answers. In these cases their results are less valid. For this reason we recommend that this measure be used as only one indicator of an individual's level of cultural intelligence.

A complete report of the development and validation of the SFCQ can be found in Thomas et al. (2015).

Notes

CHAPTER I

1. Our definition of globalization is drawn from our colleague Barbara Parker's work on this topic, 1998.

2. For insight as to what the dominant culture in the future might be, see Zakaria, 2008.

3. See Ritzer, 2008.

4. For more on this topic, see Smith & Bond, 1999.

5. For example, see the following: Hofstede, 1980; Schwartz, 1992; Trompenaars, 1993; and Triandis, 1972.

6. While this concept has gone by various names over the years, including intercultural competence, global mindset, and global competencies, the definition of the idea as a special type of intelligence can be attributed to Chris Earley in his 2002 article and in his 2003 book with Soon Ang.

7. Recently several approaches to measuring cultural intelligence have been developed. A measure of cultural intelligence as defined in this book has been developed by an international consortium of researchers called The Cultural Intelligence Project. The short form of this instrument is presented in the appendix.

8. *Mindfulness* as used in this book is conceptually equivalent to the construct called *cultural metacognition* in the academic literature.

CHAPTER 2

1. Adapted from Cushner & Brislin, 1996.
2. See Thomas et al., 2008.
3. Hofstede, 1980.
4. For an interesting discussion of organizational culture, see Deal & Kennedy, 1982.
5. For more information on the process of acculturation, see Berry, 1990.
6. Psychologists are just beginning to fully understand these so-called *bicultural* individuals. For examples of this research, see Benet-Martínez et al., 2006; and Fu et al., 2007.
7. Recent research suggests that the development of higher-order cognitive processes may be different depending on how individuals manage their multiple cultural identities. See Brannen et al., 2008.
8. The metaphor of an iceberg to represent culture comes from Schein, 1985.
9. The idea of tight and loose cultures comes from Pelto, 1968. See also Gelfand et al., 2011.
10. For a more complete discussion of convergence versus divergence of culture, see Smith and Bond, 1999; and Ralston et al., 1997.
11. For more on recontextualization, see Brannen, 2004.
12. Some researchers suggest that we can better describe cultures as being in states of multiple stable equilibriums because of the interaction of culture with other aspects of the environment. See Cohen, 2001.
13. The dimensions of individualism and collectivism have been used to explain and predict a diverse array of social behavior. However, some scholars have suggested that they have been overused and that other dimensions have been neglected. For example, see Earley & Gibson, 1998.
14. An extensive review of the causes and consequences of individualism and collectivism, including the relationship to affluence, family structure, health, religion, and politics, is contained in Triandis, 1995.
15. For additional information about these dimensions of culture, how they were derived, and the process of creating Figure 2.2, see Sagiv, 1995; Schwartz, 1992; Schwartz, 1994; and Schwartz & Bilsky, 1990.

16. See House et al., 2004.

17. See Peterson & Smith, 1997.

18. GLOBE value scores corrected for social desirability bias as reported in House et al., 2004.

CHAPTER 3

1. For more information on psychological scripts, see Abelson, 1981; Gioa & Poole, 1984; and Lord & Kernan, 1987.

2. Mindfulness is a concept that originated in Zen Buddhism. To learn more about the concept from this perspective, see the writings of the Buddhist monk Thích Nhất Hạnh, 1999 and 1991. Mindfulness was introduced into psychology literature by Langer, 1989, in her excellent book. Here we use the term more broadly to encompass what is called cultural metacognition in the academic literature. See Thomas et al., 2006, for more information.

3. The role models that are appropriate vary from culture to culture and are affected by such things as social class and gender. For example, it is much more appropriate for a young U.S. woman to model herself after a business executive than it would be for a Japanese woman to do so, and a tennis player would be a more desirable role model for an upper-class English boy than would a football (soccer) player.

4. The section on how culture affects behavior draws heavily on Thomas & Peterson, 2015.

5. Our approach to treating stereotypes as a natural outcome of social categorization is consistent with classic work on this topic. For example, see Ashmore & Del Boca, 1981.

6. Without wishing in any way to ignore or diminish the dreadful effects of racism in many countries around the world, in this book we assume that our readers do not harbor racist attitudes. That is, they acknowledge differences between groups but do not assume these differences imply superiority or inferiority. They may experience lack of understanding of other cultures and sometimes puzzlement, apprehension, even fear. But they do not feel antagonism, and to the extent that they do, they seek to overcome it. In this book we are assuming that readers have moved beyond the negative attitudes of racism and genuinely seek to manifest their recognition of the equality of all groups and their goodwill toward others in bet-

ter understanding of these groups and improving relationships with them. Also, we recognize race is not really a physical category but a social construction (see Montagu, 1942). Realizing the inadequacy of the term, we (like many scholars) use it here as shorthand to refer to genetically induced variation in humans.

7. Adapted from Cushner & Brislin, 1996.

8. For a classic description of what managers do, see Mintzberg, 1973.

9. The idea of a repertoire of behaviors as a way to define the behavioral component of cultural intelligence resulted from numerous discussions with members of the International Organizations Network (ION), particularly Allan Bird, Mark Mendenhall, Joyce Osland, Nakiye Boyacigiller, and Schon Beechlor.

10. For more information on these skills, see Thomas et al., 2008; and Thomas & Fitzsimmons, 2008.

CHAPTER 4

1. For additional information on rational decision making in management and its limitations, see Bazerman, 1998.

2. For an example of two decision models, see Nisbett et al., 2001.

3. The problems associated with rational models presented here are based on the concept of bounded rationality. See March, 1978.

4. See Lindblom, 1959.

5. The notion of heuristics presented here is derived from a classic article by Tversky & Kahneman, 1980.

6. See March, 1978; March & Simon, 1958.

7. Maier, 1970.

8. These motivational biases are based on the effects of differences in the self-concepts of culturally different individuals. See, for example, Erez & Earley, 1993.

9. Bontempo, Lobel, and Triandis, 1990.

10. See, for example, Heine & Lehman, 1995; and Miyamoto & Ktayama, 2002.

11. Adapted from a case by Shekshnia & Puffer, 2003.

12. *Guanxi* is often translated as a network of relationships. It is, however, an indigenous Chinese construct that can

only be properly understood within the Chinese context. See, for example, Gold et al., 2002.

13. Shackleton & Newell, 1994.

14. Pork barrel is a North American metaphor for the use of government funds for projects designed to please voters or legislators and win votes.

15. For more information on this central ethical question, see Donaldson, 1989.

16. The idea of a set of fundamental human rights that are invariant across cultures is central to moving beyond cultural relativism. See Donaldson, 1989; and Donaldson, 1996.

CHAPTER 5

1. Some vignettes condensed from cases by Cushner & Brislin, 1996.

2. The idea of cultural grounding in communication comes from Clark & Brennan, 1991.

3. Estimates of the number of languages in the world vary between two thousand and ten thousand. However, the number in use by significant numbers of people is many fewer. In many countries there are at least two native languages, and in some cases, such as Papua New Guinea, there are hundreds.

4. The question of the optimal age to learn a foreign language has long been studied. For more information, see Asher & Garcia, 1969. There is little debate, however, about the fact that children pick up new languages naturally while older learners generally have to struggle long and hard to achieve even moderate fluency.

5. See, for example, Giles et al., 1973.

6. See Felson, 1978.

7. Adapted from a case in Thomas & Peterson, 2014. See also, the *Japan Times*, http://www.japantimes.co.jp/opinion/2015/05/23/editorials/rakuten-forges-ahead-english/#.V2AzFCMrI6V.

8. For more information on this see Neeley, 2012.

9. This example taken from an interesting, informative, and humorous look at the English language by Bill Bryson, 2001.

10. This list of second-language strategies is adapted from Adler & Kiggundu, 1983.

11. Engholm, 1991.

12. The idea of social distance or, as it is also called, prox-emics, is drawn from Hall, 1966.

13. See, for example, Andersen & Bowman, 1985; and Aronoff et al., 1992.

14. Ekman, 1982.

15. Graham, 1987.

16. See Gelfand & McCusker, 2002, 292–314.

CHAPTER 6

1. While this is a Western definition of leadership (see Yukl, 1994), some international consensus seems to be building toward this definition. See House et al., 1997, 535–625.

2. As appealing as the idea may be, certain characteristics of individuals that are consistently related to leader emergence or leader effectiveness have not been validated by the research. For more on this topic, see Dorfman, 1996, 276–349.

3. See Dorfman, 1996.

4. Al-Kubaisy, 1985.

5. Nakane, 1970.

6. Drucker, 1994.

7. Sorge, 1993, 65–87.

8. See Puffer, 1994.

9. Management by Objectives (MBO) is a management technique based on the findings of goal-setting theory. For more information on this topic, see Locke & Latham, 1984.

10. Adapted from an unpublished case by Stanislav V. Shekshnia.

11. For more about Carlos Ghosn, see an interview with him in Stahl & Brannen, 2013.

12. For more information on paternalism see Aycan, 2008, 219–238.

13. See for example, Casey, 1999.

14. This case is adapted from Shepherd, 2003.

15. For more information on transformational leadership, see Bass, 1985; and Conger & Kanungo, 1988.

16. For example, see House et al., 1997.

17. For an example of this effect, see Thomas & Ravlin, 1995.

CHAPTER 7

1. For more information on group processes, see Goodman et al., 1987; and Hackman, 1991.
2. Arrow & McGrath, 1995.
3. Janis, 1982.
4. Mullen & Baumeister, 1987.
5. This classic experiment is described in Ringelman, 1913.
6. Process losses among individualists and collectivists also involve the extent to which the group members believe they are interacting with their in-group. For more on this topic, see Earley, 1989; and Earley, 1993.
7. The three avenues of cultural influence on groups is described in more detail in Thomas et al., 1996.
8. For a summary of this research, see Goodman et al., 1986.
9. Nemeth, 1992.
10. For a more complete description of the effects of cultural distance, see Thomas & Peterson, 2014.
11. Pearce & Ravlin, 1987.
12. Based on Allport, 1954.
13. This case was adapted from Maznevski & Chudoba, 2000.
14. For more information on this emerging topic, see an excellent book edited by Gibson & Cohen, 2003.

CHAPTER 8

1. For additional information on the inadequacy of stereotypes and the need to understand them in context, see an excellent article by Osland & Bird, 2003.
2. This diagram is adapted from an idea first presented in an excellent book on global strategy by Govindarajan & Gupta, 2001.
3. The concept of social learning was introduced by Albert Bandura. For a more extensive discussion, see Bandura, 1977.
4. Adapted from a case by Govindarajan & Gupta (2001, 126) and from the experiences of our colleague Mary Yoko Brannen.
5. Used with permission of Kayoko Takeuchi.
6. Adapted from a case in Napier & Thomas, 2004.
7. The idea that all expatriates go through a U-curve of

adjustment was first presented in Lysgaard, 1955; and Gulla-horn & Gullahorn, 1963. However, recent research has suggested that this pattern of adjustment may be far from universal. See Black & Mendenhall, 1991.

8. Case adapted from McNulty & Inkson, 2013.

9. Case adapted from Inkson & Myers, 2003.

10. From *Global Giving Matters*, September–October 2004; Pless et al., 2011; and PwC website.

11. For more information on managing expatriates see McNulty & Inkson, 2013.

Bibliography

Abelson, R. (1981). Psychological status of the script concept. *American Psychologist,* 36, 715–729.

Adler, N., & Kiggundu, M. (1983). Awareness at the crossroads: Designing translator-based training programs. In D. Landis & R. Brislin (Eds.), *Handbook of intercultural training.* Elmsford, NY: Pergamon Press.

Al-Kubaisy, A. (1985). A model in the administrative development of Arab Gulf countries. *The Arab Gulf,* 17 (2), 29–48.

Andersen, P., & Bowman, L. (1985). Positions of power: Nonverbal cues of status and dominance in organizational communication. Paper presented at the annual convention of the International Communication Association, Honolulu, HI.

Aronoff, J., Woike, B., & Hyman, L. (1992). Which are the stimuli in facial displays of anger and happiness? *Journal of Personality and Social Psychology,* 62, 1050–1066.

Arrow, H., & McGrath, J. (1993). Membership matters: How member change and continuity affect small group structure, process, and performance. *Small Group Research,* 24, 334–361.

———. (1995). Membership dynamics in groups at work: A theoretical framework. *Research in Organizational Behavior,* 17, 373–411.

Asher, J., & Garcia, R. (1969). The optimal age to learn a foreign language. *Modern Language Journal, 53*, 334–341.

Ashmore, R., & Del Boca, F. (1981). Conceptual approaches to stereotypes and stereotyping. In D. Hamilton (Ed.), *Cognitive processes in stereotyping and intergroup behavior* (pp. 1–35). Hillsdale, NJ: Erlbaum.

Aycan, Z. (2008). Cross-cultural approaches to leadership. In P. Smith, M. Peterson, & D. Thomas (Eds.), *Handbook of cross-cultural management research* (pp. 219–238). Thousand Oaks, CA: SAGE.

Bandura, A. (1977). *Social learning theory.* Englewood Cliffs, NJ: Prentice-Hall.

Bartlett, C., & Ghoshal, S. (1989). *Managing across borders: The transnational solution.* Boston: Harvard Business School Press.

Bass, B. (1985). *Leadership and performance beyond expectation.* New York: Free Press.

Bazerman, M. (1998). *Judgement in managerial decision making,* 4th Edition. New York: John Wiley & Sons.

Berry, J. (1990). The psychology of acculturation: Understanding individuals moving between cultures. In R. Brislin (Ed.), *Cross-cultural research and methodology series: Vol. 14. Applied cross-cultural psychology* (pp. 232–252). Newbury Park, CA: SAGE.

Black, J., & Mendenhall, M. (1991). The U-curve adjustment hypothesis revisited: A review and theoretical framework. *Journal of International Business Studies, 22*, 225–247.

Bontempo, R., Lobel, S., & Triandis, H. (1990). Compliance and value internalization in Brazil and the U.S.: Effects of allocentrism and anonymity. *Journal of Cross-Cultural Psychology, 21*, 200–213.

Brannen, M. (2004). When Mickey loses face: Recontextualization, semantic fit, and the semiotics of foreignness. *Academy of Management Review, 29* (4), 593–616.

Brannen, M., Garcia, D., & Thomas, D. (2008). The impact of biculturalism on cross-cultural cognitive and behavioral skills. Paper presented to the annual Meeting of the Academy of Management, Anaheim, CA.

Bryson, B. (2001). *The mother tongue: English and how it got that way.* New York: HarperCollins.

Casey, C. (1999). Come join our family: Discipline and integration in corporate organization cultures. *Human Relations,* 52 (2), 155–178.

Catlin, L., & White, T. (2001). *International business: Cultural sourcebook and case studies.* Cincinnati, OH: South-Western College Publishing.

Clark, H., & Brennan, S. (1991). Grounding in communication. *Perspectives on Socially Shared Communication.* Washington, DC: American Psychological Association.

Cohen, D. (2001). Cultural variation: Consideration and implications. *Psychological Bulletin,* 127, 451–471.

Conger, J., & Kanungo, R. (1988). *Charismatic leadership: The elusive factor in organizational effectiveness.* San Francisco: Jossey-Bass.

Cushner, K., & Brislin, R. (1996). *Intercultural interactions: A practical guide.* Thousand Oaks, CA: SAGE.

Deal, T., & Kennedy, A. (1982). *Corporate culture: The rites and rituals of corporate life.* Reading, MA: Addison-Wesley.

DiStefano, J. (2003). Johannes Bosch sends an e-mail. In D. Thomas (Ed.), *Readings and cases in international management: A cross-cultural perspective* (pp. 347–350). Thousand Oaks, CA: SAGE Publications.

Donaldson, T. (1989). *The ethics of international business.* New York: Oxford University Press.

———. (1996). Values in tension: Ethics away from home. *Harvard Business Review,* Sept./Oct., 48–62.

Dorfman, P. (1996). International and cross-cultural leadership. In B. Punnitt & O. Shenkar (Eds.), *Handbook for international management research* (pp. 276–349). Cambridge, MA: Blackwell.

Dorfman, P., & Howell, J. (1988). Dimensions of national culture and effective leadership patterns: Hofstede revisited. *Advances in international comparative management,* 3, 127–150.

Drucker, P. (1994). The new superpower: The overseas Chinese. *Wall Street Journal* (December 20), 17.

Earley, P. C. (1989). Social loafing and collectivism: A comparison of the U.S. and the People's Republic of China. *Administrative Science Quarterly,* 34, 565–581.

———. (1993). East meets West meets Mid-East: Further explorations of collectivistic and individualistic work groups. *Academy of Management Journal*, 36, 319–348.

———. (2002). Redefining interactions across cultures and organizations: Moving forward with cultural intelligence. *Research in Organizational Behavior*, 24, 271–299.

Earley, P., & Ang, S. (2003). *Cultural intelligence: Individual interactions across cultures.* Stanford, CA: Stanford University Press.

Earley, P., & Gibson, C. (1998). Taking stock in our progress on individualism-collectivism: 100 years of solidarity and community. *Journal of Management*, 24, 265–304.

Ekman, P. (1982). *Emotion in the human face,* 2nd Edition. Cambridge: Cambridge University Press.

Engholm, C. (1991). *When business East meets business West: The guide to practice and protocol in the Pacific rim.* New York: Wiley.

Erez, M., & Earley, P. (1987). Comparative analysis of goal setting strategies across cultures. *Journal of Applied Psychology*, 71, 658–665.

———. (1993). *Culture, self-identity, and work.* New York: Oxford University Press.

Felson, R. (1978). Aggression is impression management. *Social Psychology Quarterly*, 41, 259–281.

Fu, J. H-Y., Chiu, C-Y., Morris, M., & Young, M. (2007). Spontaneous inferences from cultural cues. Varying responses of cultural insiders and outsiders. *Journal of Cross-Cultural Psychology*, 38, 58–75.

Gelfand, M., & McCusker, C. (2002). Metaphor and cultural construction of negotiation: A paradigm for research and practice. In M. Gannon and K. Newman (Eds.), *Handbook of cross-cultural management* (pp. 292–314). Malden, MA: Blackwell.

Gibson, C., & Cohen, S. (Eds.) (2003). *Virtual teams that work: Creating conditions for virtual team effectiveness.* San Francisco: Jossey-Bass.

Giles, H., Taylor, D., & Bourhis, R. (1973). Towards a theory of interpersonal accommodation through language: Some Canadian data. *Language in Society*, 2, 177–192.

Gioa, D., & Poole, P. (1984). Scripts in organizational behavior. *Academy of Management Review*, 9, 449–459.

Gold, T., Guthrie, D., & Wank, D. (Eds.) (2002). *Social connections in China: Institutions, culture, and the changing nature of Guanxi.* Cambridge: Cambridge University Press.

Goodman, P., Ravlin, E., & Argote, L. (1986). Current thinking about groups: Setting the stage for new ideas. In P. Goodman (Ed.), *Designing effective work groups.* San Francisco: Jossey-Bass.

Goodman, P., Ravlin, E., & Schminke, M. (1987). Understanding groups in organizations. In B. Staw & L. Cummings (Eds.), *Research in organizational behavior* (Vol. 9, pp. 124–128). Greenwich, CT: JAI Press.

Govindarajan, V., & Gupta, A. (2001). *The quest for global dominance.* San Francisco: Jossey-Bass.

Graham, J. (1987). A theory of interorganizational negotiations. *Research in Marketing, 9,* 163–183.

Gullahorn, J., & Gullahorn, J. (1963). An extension of the U-curve hypothesis. *Journal of Social Issues, 19,* 33–47.

Hackman, J. (1991). *Groups that work (and those that don't).* San Francisco: Jossey-Bass.

Hall, E. (1966). *The hidden dimension.* Garden City, NY: Doubleday.

Heine, S., & Lehman, D. (1995). Cultural variation in unrealistic optimism: Does the West feel more invulnerable than the East? *Journal of Personality and Social Psychology, 68,* 595–607.

Hofstede, G. (1980). *Culture's consequences: International differences in work related values.* Beverly Hills, CA: SAGE.

House, R., Hanges, P., Javidan, M., Dorfman, P., & Gupta, V. (2004). *Culture, leadership, and organizations: The GLOBE study of 62 societies.* Thousand Oaks, CA: SAGE.

House, R., Wright, N., & Aditya, R. (1997). Cross-cultural research on organizational leadership: A critical analysis and a proposed theory. In P. Earley & M. Erez (Eds.), *New Perspectives on international industrial/organizational psychology* (pp. 535–625). San Francisco: New Lexington Press.

Inkson, K., & Myers, B. (2003). "The big O.E.": International travel and career development. *Career Development International, 8* (4), 170–181.

Janis, I. (1982). *Groupthink.* Boston: Houghton Mifflin.

Kuhn, M., & McPartland, T. (1954). An empirical investigation of self-attitudes. *American Sociological Review*, 19 (1), 68–76.

Lane, H., DiStefano, J., & Maznevski, M. (2000). *International management behavior: Text, readings and cases*. Malden, MA: Blackwell.

Langer, E. (1989). *Mindfulness*. Cambridge, MA: Perseus Books.

Lindblom, C. (1959). The science of muddling through. *Public Administration Review*, 19 (2), 278–294.

Locke, E., & Latham, G. (1984). *Goal setting: A motivational technique that works*. Englewood Cliffs, NJ: Prentice-Hall.

Lord, R., & Kernan, M. (1987). Scripts as determinants of purposeful behavior in organizations. *Academy of Management Review*, 12, 265–277.

Lysgaard, S. (1955). Adjustment in a foreign society: Norwegian Fulbright grantees visiting the United States. *International Social Science Bulletin*, 7, 45–51.

Maier, N. (1970). *Problem solving and creativity in individuals and groups*. Belmont, CA: Brookes/Cole.

March, J. (1978). Bounded rationality, ambiguity, and the engineering of choice. *Bell Journal of Economics*, 9 (2), 587–608.

March, J., & Simon, H. (1958). *Organizations*. New York: Wiley.

Maznevski, M., & Chudoba, K. (2000). Bridging space over time: Global virtual team dynamics and effectiveness. *Organization Science*, 11 (5), 473–492.

McLuhan, M. (1962). *The Gutenberg galaxy*. Toronto: University of Toronto Press.

———. (1964). *Understanding media: The extensions of man*. New York: McGraw-Hill.

McNulty, Y., & Inkson, K. (2013). *Managing expatriates: A return on investment approach*. New York: Business Expert Press.

Mendenhall, M., Lane, H., Maznevski, M., & McNett, J. (Eds.). (2003). *Handbook of cross-cultural management*. Oxford: Blackwell.

Mintzberg, H. (1973). *The nature of managerial work*. New York: Harper & Row.

Miyamoto, Y., & Ktayama, S. (2002). Cultural variation in correspondence bias: The critical role of attitude diagnosticity and socially constrained behavior. *Journal of Personality and Social Psychology*, 83 (5), 1239–1248.

Mullen, B., & Baumeister R. (1987). Groups effects on self-attention and performance: Social loafing, social facilitation, and social impairment. In C. Hendrick (Ed.), *Review of personality and social psychology* (pp. 189–206). Newbury Park, CA: SAGE.

Nakane, C. (1970). *Japanese society.* Berkeley: University of California Press.

Napier, N., & Thomas, D. (2004). *Managing relationships in transition economies.* New York: Praeger.

Neeley, T. (2012). Global business speaks English. *Harvard Business Review*, 90 (5), 116–124.

Nemeth, C. (1992). Minority dissent as a stimulant to group performance. In S. Worchel, W. Wood, & J. Simpson (Eds.), *Group process and productivity* (pp. 95–111). Newbury Park, CA: SAGE.

The new webster encyclopedic dictionary of the english language. (1971). Chicago: Consolidated Book Publishers.

Nisbett, R. E., Peng, K., Choi, I., & Norenzayan, A. (2001). Culture and systems of thought: Holistic versus analytic cognition. *Psychological Review*, 108 (2), 291–310.

Nisbett, R., & Ross, L. (1980). *Human inference.* Englewood Cliffs, NJ: Prentice-Hall.

Osland, J., & Bird, A. (2003). Beyond sophisticated stereotyping: Cultural sensemaking in context. In D. Thomas (Ed.), *Readings and cases in international management: A cross-cultural perspective* (pp. 58–70). Thousand Oaks, CA: SAGE Publications.

Parker, B. (1998). *Globalization: Managing across boundaries.* London: SAGE.

Pearce, J., & Ravlin, E. (1987). The design and activation of self-regulating work groups. *Human Relations*, 11, 751–782.

Pelto, P. (1968). The difference between tight and loose societies. *Transaction*, April, 37–40.

Peterson, M., & Smith, P. B. (1997). Does national culture or ambient temperature explain cross-cultural differences in role stress? *Academy of Management Journal*, 40, 930–946.

Pless, N. M., Maak, T., & Stahl, G. K. (2011). Developing responsible global leaders through international service-learning programs. *Academy of Management Learning & Education*, 10 (2), 237–260.

Puffer, S. (1994). A portrait of Russian business leaders. *Academy of Management Executive*, 8 (1), 41–54.

Ralston, D., Holt, D., Terpstra, R., & Yu, K. (1997). The impact of national culture and economic ideology on managerial work values: A study of the United States, Russia, Japan, and China. *Journal of International Business Studies*, 28 (1), 177–207.

Ringelman, M. (1913). Recherches sur les moteurs animes: Travails de l'homme. *Annales de l'Institut Nationale Agronomique*, 12, 1–40.

Ritzer, G. (2008). *The McDonaldization of Society 5*. Thousand Oaks, CA: Pine Forge Press.

Roberts, K., & Boyacigiller, N. (1984). Cross-national organizational research: The grasp of the blind men. In B. Staw & L. Cummings (Eds.), *Research in organizational behavior* (Vol. 6, pp. 423–475). Greenwich, CT: JAI Press.

Sagiv, L., & Schwartz, S. (1995). Value priorities and readiness for outgroup social contact. *Journal of Personality and Social Psychology*, 69, 437–448.

Schein, E. (1985). *Organizational culture and leadership*. San Francisco: Jossey-Bass.

Schwartz, S. (1992). Universals in the content and structure of values: Theoretical advances and empirical tests in 20 countries. In M. Zanna (Ed.), *Advances in Experimental Social Psychology* (pp. 1–65). San Diego: Academic Press.

———. (1994). Beyond individualism/collectivism: New dimensions of values. In U. Kim, H. Triandis, C. Kagitçibasi, S. Choi, and G. Yoon (Eds.), *Individualism and collectivism: Theory, applications, and methods* (pp. 85–119). Newbury Park, CA: SAGE.

Schwartz, S., & Bilsky, W. (1990). Toward a universal psychological structure of human values. *Journal of Personality and Social Psychology*, 53, 550–562.

Shackleton, V., & Newell, S. (1994). European management

selection methods: A comparison of five countries. *International Journal of Selection and Assessment*, 2, 91–102.

Shekshnia, S., & Puffer, S. (2003). Rus Wane equipment: Joint venture in Russia. In D. Thomas (Ed.), *Readings and cases in international management: A cross-cultural perspective* (pp. 254–266). Thousand Oaks, CA, SAGE Publications.

Shepherd, D. (2003). Common bond values at the New Zealand office of AT&T. In D. Thomas (Ed.), *Readings and cases in international management: A cross-cultural perspective* (pp. 92–100). Thousand Oaks, CA: SAGE Publications.

Smith, P., & Bond, M. (1999). *Social psychology across cultures*. Boston: Allyn and Bacon.

Sorge, A. (1993). Management in France. In D. Hickson (Ed.), *Management in Western Europe: Society, culture and organization in twelve nations* (pp. 65–87). New York: Walter de Gruyter.

Stahl, G., & Branne, M. Y. (2013). Building cross cultural leadership competence: An interview with Carlos Ghosn. *Academy of Management Learning & Education*, 12 (3), 494–502.

Thích Nhất Hạnh. (1991). *Peace is every step: The path of mindfulness in everyday life*. New York: Bantam Books.

———. (1999). *The miracle of mindfulness*. Boston: Beacon Press.

Thomas, D. (1998). The expatriate experience: A critical review and synthesis. *Advances in International Comparative Management*, 12, 237–273.

———. (2008). *Cross-cultural management: Essential concepts*. Thousand Oaks, CA: SAGE.

———, (Ed.). (2003). *Readings and cases in international management: A cross-cultural perspective*. Thousand Oaks, CA: SAGE.

Thomas, D. C., & Fitzsimmons, S. R. (2008). Cross-cultural skills and abilities: From communication competence to cultural intelligence. In P. B. Smith, M. F. Peterson, and D. C. Thomas (Eds.), *The handbook of cross-cultural management research*. Thousand Oaks, CA: SAGE.

Thomas, D., Liao, Y., Ayçan, Z., Cerdin, J-L., Pekerti, A., Ravlin, E., Stahl, G., Lazarova, M., Fock, H., Arli, D., Moeller, M., Okimoto, T., & van de Vijver, F. (2015). Cultural intelligence: A theory-based, short form measure. *Journal of International Business Studies, 46* (9), 1099–1118.

Thomas, D., & Peterson, M. (2015). *Cross-cultural management: Essential concepts*, 3rd Edition. Thousand Oaks, CA: SAGE.

Thomas, D., & Ravlin, E. (1995). Responses of employees to cultural adaptation by a foreign manager. *Journal of Applied Psychology*, 80, 133–146.

Thomas, D., Au, K., & Ravlin, E. (2003). Cultural variation and the psychological contract. *Journal of Organizational Behavior*, 24, 451–471.

Thomas, D., Ravlin, E., & Wallace, A. (1996). Effect of cultural diversity in work groups. *Research in Sociology of Organizations*, 14, 1–33.

Thomas, D., Stahl, G., Ravlin, E., Pekerti, A., Poelmans, S., Maznevski, M., Lazarova, M., Elron, E., Ekelund, B., Cerdin, J-L., Brislin, R., Aycan, Z., Au, K. (2008). Cultural intelligence: Domain and assessment. *International Journal of Cross-Cultural Management*, 8 (2), 123–143.

Triandis, H. (1972). *The analysis of subjective culture*. New York: Wiley.

———. (1995). *Individualism and collectivism*. Boulder, CO: Westview.

Trompenaars, F. (1993). *Riding the waves of culture*. Burr Ridge, IL: Irwin.

Tuckman, B. (1965). Developmental sequence in small groups. *Psychological Bulletin*, 63 (6), 384–399.

Tversky, A., & Kahneman, D. (1980). Judgement under uncertainty: Heuristics and biases. *Science*, 85, 1124–1131.

Walker, R. (1999). Picnic in Samoa. In N. Monin, J. Monin, & R. Walker (Eds.), *Narratives of business and society: Differing New Zealand voices* (pp. 143–153). Auckland: Longman.

Yukl, G. (1994). *Leadership in organizations,* 3rd Edition. Upper Saddle River, NJ: Prentice-Hall.

Zakaria, F. (2008). *The post-American world*. New York: W. W. Norton.

Index

Behavioral cues, 55
Bicultural individuals, 170n6
Body language. *See* Nonverbal
    communication
Body position, 89–90
Brazil, as example of collectivist
    behavior, 66
Bribery, 70
Bumbacea, Dinu, 155

Canada
    cultural characteristics of, 26,
        145–146
    as culturally similar to New
        Zealand, 32
    as culturally similar to United
        States, 73
Celtic peoples, 47
Charismatic leadership, 113
China
    guanxi in, 68, 173n12
    high expatriate failure rate,
        148
Chinese language, 148
Chinese people, 147–148,
    150–151
    business practices, 3–4
    customs, 18–19
    leadership behavior, 104
    respect for authority, 27
    scripts, 42
    values, 25
Christian culture, 24
Churchill, Winston, 113
Collectivism, 30–31. *See also*
    Individualism
    as basis for communication
        conventions, 84–85
    as basis for generalizations
        about cultures, 115
    as influential in teams, 123
    as limitation in rational
        decision making, 65
Collectivist(ic) cultures. *See*

also High- and low-context
    cultures
    characteristics, 30, 109
    decision making in, 66–67,
        69
    leader behavior in, 109
    members in groups, 118–119
    motivation in, 100, 101
    rewards in, 128
    selective perception in, 46
Communication. *See also*
    Language
    defined, 77–78
    explicit vs. implicit, 84–85
    failures in, 48, 77
    silence in, 76–78, 85–86, 99
Communication codes, 77–78,
    96
Communication conventions,
    78–80, 84–86, 96
Communication skills, 20
Context in which words are
    spoken. *See* High- and low-
    context cultures
Convergence, cultural, 12,
    27–28
CQ. *See* Cultural intelligence
Crew, as type of work group,
    121, 122, 134
Cross-cultural adjustment,
    U-curve of, 148–149, 149f
Cross-cultural communication,
    principles for, 95–96
Cross-cultural communication
    process, 79, 80f
Cross-cultural differences. *See*
    Cultural difference
Cross-cultural engagement,
    rules of, 157–158
Cross-cultural skills, 41,
    51–55. *See also* Skilled
    performance
    developing, 96
Cruise control, cultural, 16,

as basis for cultural generalizations, 115
as characteristic of Westerners, 118
in communication conventions, 84
as influential in teams, 123
Individualist(ic) cultures. *See also* High- and low-context cultures
characteristics of, 30
decision making in, 65, 66–67, 69
direct communication convention in, 84
group members in, 118–119
groupthink in, 124
leadership behavior in, 109
motivation in, 100, 101
rewards in, 128–129
selective perception in, 46
Institutional collectivism, 34, 36t
Intellectual autonomy, 32
Intelligence quotient (IQ), x, 15
Intercultural families, 10–11
Interdependent effort of group members, 130
International business environment, 16–17
characteristics, 7
International travel. *See also* Foreign experience and expatriate assignments
acquiring cultural intelligence through, 154–157
Irish people, stereotypes of, 47
Islam, leadership and, 103

Japan
arbitration model of decision making in, 94
English language use in, 82–83

leader behavior in, 100, 104
nonverbal behavior in, 90
as similar to United States on mastery, 32
as a tight culture, 26
Japanese people
in-group behavior, 48
judgment in decision making, 66
selective perception, 48
silence as negotiation tactic, 85–86

Kennedy, John F., 113
Krall, Diana, 55, 56
Kurdi, Alan "Aylan," 6

Language, 28. *See also* English language
as characteristic of culture, 25
a common organizational, 82–84
in communication, 1–3, 99–101
as means of social categorization, 46
in negotiation, 162
Language codes, finding common, 81
Language skills, 96–97
Language standardization. *See* Language: a common organizational
Laundry list, as approach to cross-cultural understanding, 13–15, 28
Leadership, 98–100
charismatic/transformational, 113
Leadership *(continued)*
culture and expectations of followers, 108–110
defined, 99
and followership, 112

in multinational organizations,
110–112
popular ideas of, 101–102
Leadership skills, 47
Leadership styles, 102–103,
115–116, 162
concern for tasks vs. concern
for relationships, 102–
103, 115

Malaysian conventions about
dress, 40–43, 52
Management by Objectives
(MBO), 106, 174n9
Management science, 61
Managerial style, 4
"Managing diversity," 111–112
Mandela, Nelson, 113
Marketing myopia. *See*
Mindlessness
Mastery, 32
McCann, Brian, 155
McDonaldization, 12
McDonald's, 27–28
Mediterranean peoples, 47
Mental maps, 161
Mental programming, 21,
23–25, 45, 75
levels of, 21–22, 22f
Mexican cultural norms, 29–30,
37–38
Mexico, cultural profile of, 37
Mianzi, 137
Mikitani, Hiroshi, 82
Mindful attention, 50, 52. *See
also* Attention
Mindful monitoring, 50
Mindful regulation, 50–51
Mindfulness, 14, 16, 19–20, 41,
49–51, 145–147, 169n8,
171n2
as component of cultural
intelligence, 138, 140
in decision making, 74

defined, 160–161
as leadership characteristic,
107, 115
in multicultural teams, 119
in negotiation, 161
practicing, 96
as principle in cross-cultural
communication, 96
Mindlessness, 43
benefits of, 43
in communication, 81
as cultural cruise control, 50–
51. *See also* Cruise control
dangers of, 43–44
example of, 43
Moral rules, 73
Motivation. *See also under*
Decision making
across cultures, 100–101
Multinational corporations
(MNC), 7, 111

Negotiating across cultures,
91–93
Negotiating styles, 94–95
Negotiation, principles for
cross-cultural, 95–96
New-Product Development
Team (NPD), 131–132
New Zealand, 76
as culturally similar to
Canada, 32
leadership in, 111–112
9/11 terrorist attacks, 5
Nonverbal communication,
86–91, 162
Norms, 36
of acceptance of group
activities, 130
in communication, 78, 84–85
cultural, 41, 56, 71, 74,
125, 138–139. *See also*
Mexican cultural norms
of employing children, 75

Self-management, in teams, 129
September 11, 2001 terrorist
    attacks, 5
Serbian people, 48
Sheikhocracy, 103
Short Form Cultural Intelligence
    Assessment (SFCQ),
    165–167
  important findings regarding,
    167–168
  using, 167
Sikhism, 145–147
Silence, 76–78, 85–86, 99
Skilled performance, 55–56. *See
    also* Cross-cultural skills
Slavs, 47
Social categorization, 46–47.
    See also Stereotypes and
    stereotyping
Social distance, in
    communication, 88–89
Social learning, 140
Social loafing, 123
Socialization, 44
Starbucks, 27
Stereotypes and stereotyping,
    19, 23, 47, 140. *See also*
    Social categorization
Subcultures, 22–23, 26
Sun Tzu, 115
Synergy, 11, 124
Syrian Civil War, refugees of
    the, 6

Task activities, 119–121
Task force, as type of work
    group, 121, 122, 134
Task-oriented leadership,
    102–103, 115
Teamwork, 52. *See also* Work
    groups and teams
Thai people, 76–78
Touching, 86–89
Trade, international, 7

Training
  cross-cultural, 147–148
  formal, 142–143
  types of, 142–143, 143t
Transformational leadership,
    113

Uncertainty
  avoidance of, 34, 37t
  tolerance for, 55
United States. *See also* American
    culture; Americans
  characteristics of leaders in,
    100
  cultural imperialism, 12, 27
  cultural profile, 37
  as culturally similar to
    Canada, 73
  as example of individualism,
    66
  example of social behavior
    in, 4
  as loose culture, 26
  as similar to Japan on mastery,
    32
  touching behavior, 89

Value dimensions across
    nations, 31–32, 33f
Values, 25
  cultural, 21–22, 27–31, 113,
    115
  culture as an organized system
    of, 24–25
  dimensions of variation in,
    29–32, 33f
  historical basis of, 140
  as part of the cultural field,
    79, 80f
  as relative to society, 73–74
  as underlying decision-making
    behavior, 75
  as way to anticipate
    differences, 95–96

About the Authors

DAVID C. THOMAS is the Beedie Professor of International Management at Simon Fraser University, Vancouver, Canada. He is the author of ten books, including *Essentials of International Human Resource Management: Managing People Globally* (with Mila Lazarova). His book *Cross-Cultural Management: Essential Concepts*, from SAGE Publications was the winner of the R. Wayne Pace Human Resource Development Book of the Year award for 2008. In addition, he has recently edited (with Peter B. Smith and Mark Peterson) *The Handbook of Cross-Cultural Management Research*, also from SAGE Publications. His research on cross-cultural interactions in organizational settings has taken him around the world, and articles based on that research have appeared in numerous journals. He has lived and worked in Australia, New Zealand, Turkey, Hong Kong, France, Canada, and the United States. In addition to teaching at both the undergraduate and postgraduate levels, Dave has developed executive education programs in Australia, New Zealand, Canada, and the United States and has served as a consultant on cultural diversity issues to a number of multinational firms and government agencies. When not writing or teaching, he can often be found scraping or varnishing (or sometimes sailing) his 1984 Hans Christian cutter, *Clovelly.*

KERR INKSON is an Emeritus Professor and Research Advisor (part-time) at the University of Auckland, New Zealand and is semi-retired. He is the author, co-author, or co-editor of twenty books, including *Theory K, The New Careers, Career Studies, Understanding Careers, Managing Expatriates,* and *Cultural Intelligence;* 75 refereed journal articles; and over 50 book chapters. His recent research has focused mainly on careers, including international careers and metaphorical representations of career. He has held academic positions in New Zealand, the United Kingdom, and the United States. He has served as a professor of management at five of New Zealand's universities and has extensive experience in consulting and executive education, including a term as director of an Executive MBA program. He runs his own small academic editing business and leads retreats and workshops enabling PhD students in business studies to improve their writing skills. Kerr lives in Auckland and is active in amateur drama.

Berrett–Koehler
Publishers

Berrett-Koehler is an independent publisher dedicated to an ambitious mission: *Connecting people and ideas to create a world that works for all.*

We believe that the solutions to the world's problems will come from all of us, working at all levels: in our organizations, in our society, and in our own lives. Our BK Business books help people make their organizations more humane, democratic, diverse, and effective (we don't think there's any contradiction there). Our BK Currents books offer pathways to creating a more just, equitable, and sustainable society. Our BK Life books help people create positive change in their lives and align their personal practices with their aspirations for a better world.

All of our books are designed to bring people seeking positive change together around the ideas that empower them to see and shape the world in a new way.

And we strive to practice what we preach. At the core of our approach is Stewardship, a deep sense of responsibility to administer the company for the benefit of all of our stakeholder groups including authors, customers, employees, investors, service providers, and the communities and environment around us. Everything we do is built around this and our other key values of quality, partnership, inclusion, and sustainability.

This is why we are both a B-Corporation and a California Benefit Corporation—a certification and a for-profit legal status that require us to adhere to the highest standards for corporate, social, and environmental performance.

We are grateful to our readers, authors, and other friends of the company who consider themselves to be part of the BK Community. We hope that you, too, will join us in our mission.

A BK Business Book

We hope you enjoy this BK Business book. BK Business books pioneer new leadership and management practices and socially responsible approaches to business. They are designed to provide you with groundbreaking and practical tools to transform your work and organizations while upholding the triple bottom line of people, planet, and profits. High-five!

To find out more, visit **www.bkconnection.com.**

Berrett–Koehler
Publishers

Connecting people and ideas
to create a world that works for all

Dear Reader,

Thank you for picking up this book and joining our worldwide community of Berrett-Koehler readers. We share ideas that bring positive change into people's lives, organizations, and society.

To welcome you, we'd like to offer you a free e-book. You can pick from among twelve of our bestselling books by entering the promotional code **BKP92E** here: http://www.bkconnection.com/welcome.

When you claim your free e-book, we'll also send you a copy of our e-newsletter, the *BK Communiqué*. Although you're free to unsubscribe, there are many benefits to sticking around. In every issue of our newsletter you'll find

- A free e-book
- Tips from famous authors
- Discounts on spotlight titles
- Hilarious insider publishing news
- A chance to win a prize for answering a riddle

Best of all, our readers tell us, "Your newsletter is the only one I actually read." So claim your gift today, and please stay in touch!

Sincerely,

Charlotte Ashlock
Steward of the BK Website

Questions? Comments? Contact me at bkcommunity@bkpub.com.

Certified

Corporation
bcorporation.net